W9-BOB-362

אֵיזֶהוּ
גִבּוֹר

EIZEHU GIBOR

LIVING JEWISH VALUES

PHOTO CREDITS: American Jewish Archives, pages 51, 97; AP Images, pages 21, 22, 37, 38; basel01658, page 16; Bechol Lashon, pages 39, 40; Giovanni Benintende, page 68; Bettmann/CORBIS, pages 28, 32, 43, 44, 46, 55, 57, 58, 87; Nikola Bilc, page 10 (foreground); Rob Byron, page 30; Brian Chase, page 92 (foreground); Michal Cizik/Gettyimages, page 54; danielsko, page 28 (background); danilo ducak, page 53 (background); Rob Dunlavey, page 23; Entertainment Press, page 93; Tom Fakler, page 12; fotoret, page 36; Gaspar Furman, page 63; Zorik Galstyan, page 71 (background); Gabrielle Gelselman, page 88; Dr. Nachum Tim Gidal/Hadassah, page 85; Mandy Godbehear, page 20 (bottom); Bernard Gotfryd/Gettyimages, page 57 (top); Hashomer Hatzair/Israelimages, page 42; Benrei Huang, page 76; Hulton-Deutsch Collection/CORBIS, page 67; Chen Ping Hung, page 5; Hanan Isachar/Israelimages, page 64; Jewish World Watch, pages 7, 8, 9; Junial Enterprises, page 56 (front); Iakov Kalinin, page 96; Elena Kalistratova, page 34; KZWW, page 32 (background); Mikhail Levit, page 66; Luis Louro, page 72; Maccabi World Union, page 19; Josh Mason-Barkin, page 15; Arkaday Mazor, page 60; Lorelyn Medina, page 70; Matthew Mendelsohn/CORBIS, page 31; Amy Meyers, page 20 (top); Michael Monahan, page 82; Murata-pho.com, page 6; Nafania, page 74; Scott Nelson/Gettyimages, page 8 (top); Cloudia Newland, page 10 (background); OJCEIV, page 17; Olly, page 83; pavelr, page 71 (front); Photosky4T.com, page 48; Raqnarock, page 56 (background); Reuters/CORBIS, page 25; Win Robins, page 41; Jörg Röse-Oberreich/Israelimages, page 47; David Rubinger, page 13; Yaakov Saar/Gettyimages, page 26; Scapes, page 24; Stephen Schildbach, page 80; Rosteckiy Sergey, page 92 (background); John S. Sfondilias, page 94; Moshe Shai/Israelimages, page 25 (top); Angie Sidles, page 18; Beth Spiegel, page 84; Josef F. Stuefer, page 14; Israel Talby/Israelimages, page 86; Tiax, page 17; Tom Uhlenberg, page 52; Ultraviolet, page 59; Underwood & Underwood/CORBIS, page 75; Veer, page 35; Tammy Veriable/Veer, page 77; Vikasun, page 53; Vladiwelt, page 29; Marilon Volan, page 11; Denis Vrublevski, page 89; Eugene Wanov, page 95; wcpmedia, page 65.

Thank you to Debbie Friedman, Craig Taubman, Rabbi Mark Borovitz, Rabbi Harold Schulweis, Janice Kamenir-Reznik and Danny Siegel for providing a photograph for their biography pages. We wish to also thank Matthew Lutts of APInternational, The American Jewish Archives and Bechol Lashon for helping us to find needed photographs.

ISBN 10: 1-934527-24-6

ISBN 13: 978-1-934527-24-5

Copyright © 2009 Torah Aura Productions. All rights reserved.

No part of this publication may be reproduced or transmitted in any form or by any means graphic, electronic or mechanical, including photocopying, recording or by any information storage and retrieval system, without permission in writing from the publisher.

Torah Aura Productions • 4423 Fruitland Avenue, Los Angeles, CA 90058

(800) BE-Torah • (800) 238-6724 • (323) 585-7312 • fax (323) 585-0327

E-MAIL <misrad@torahaura.com> • Visit the Torah Aura website at www.torahaura.com

MANUFACTURED IN CHINA

contents

tikkun olam 5
   Rabbi Harold M. Schulweis 7
   Janice Kamenir-Reznik 8

shmirat ha-teva 11
   David Ben-Gurion 13
   Kibbutz Lotan 15

shmirat ha-guf 17
   The Maccabiah Games 19
   Lenny Krayzelburg 21

rodef shalom 23
   Yitzhak Rabin 25
   The Four Chaplains 27

zikaron 29
   Elie Wiesel 31
   Dov Noy 33

kol yisrael arevim zeh ba-zeh 35
   Robert and Myra Kraft 37
   Gershom Sizomu 39

tzionut 41
   Theodor Herzl 43
   Golda Meir 45

ometz lev 47
   Rabbi Regina Jonas 49
   Rabbi Leo Baeck 51

tzedek tzedek tirdof 53
   Justice Louis Brandeis 55
   Rabbi Abraham Joshua Heschel 57

t'shuvah 59
   Rabbi Mark Borovitz 61
   John Paul II 63

anavah 65
    Albert Einstein 67
    Moses 69

kiddush ha-shem 71
    Hannah Szenes 73
    Hank Greenberg 75

shiru l'adonai 77
    Debbie Friedman 79
    Craig Taubman 81

pikuah nefesh 83
    Henrietta Szold 85
    Jonas Salk 87

tzedakah 89
    Danny Siegel 91
    Natalie Portman 93

talmud torah 95
    Rebecca Gratz 97
    Nehama Leibowitz 99

tikkun olam

Tikkun olam means "fixing the world". The world is broken. There is hunger, racism, war, slavery, prejudice, poverty, and lots of other problems. Because we are created in God's image, because we are God's partners, it is our job to solve these problems.

A rabbi by the name of Isaac Luria (1534–1572) told a story that the world God created is not finished. There is work left to do. The job of finishing creation and fixing the world is left to us. *Tikkun olam* is our responsibility. We can't ask God to do things we can accomplish ourselves.

Tikkun olam is building a home for the homeless. It is feeding the hungry and tutoring those who need help in learning. It is making sure that everyone is safe. It is ending prejudice and discrimination. It is making the world the best it can be. *Tikkun olam* teaches us that our responsibilities go beyond ourselves and our families. We are responsible for our community, other communities—the whole world. In the Talmud, in a book called *Pirkei Avot*, Rabbi Tarfon taught, "You are not required to finish the job, neither are you free to neglect it." This means "You are not required to do everything the world needs, but never are you allowed to quit working on it."

tikkun olam text: aleinu

One of the final prayers in most Jewish services is the *Aleinu*. From it we learn about *tikkun olam*. This is from a paragraph that is usually said silently or not included in the prayerbook.

עַל כֵּן נְקַוֶּה לְךָ יי אֱלֹהֵינוּ...
לְתַקֵּן עוֹלָם בְּמַלְכוּת שַׁדַּי
וְכָל־בְּנֵי בָשָׂר יִקְרְאוּ בִשְׁמֶךָ, לְהַפְנוֹת אֵלֶיךָ...
וְתִמְלֹךְ עֲלֵיהֶם מְהֵרָה לְעוֹלָם וָעֶד.

We therefore put our hope in You, Eternal our God...
(For us) to do *tikkun olam* under the leadership of the Eternal
And all people will call Your Name and turn back to You...
And You will reign over them, soon, and forever and ever.

1. What does *tikkun olam* mean in this prayer?
2. What does God have to do to create *tikkun olam*?
3. What do people have to do to create *tikkun olam*?
4. What does "and all people will call Your Name" have to do with *tikkun olam*?

rabbi harold schulweis

Rabbi Harold Schulweis is one of the most famous rabbis in America. He is a rabbi at Valley Beth Shalom, a Conservative congregation in Encino, California. Rabbi Schulweis was born in the Bronx, New York, to parents who respected Zionism and Jewish traditions. His early Jewish education was shaped by his grandfather, Rabbi Avraham Rezak, who introduced him to the Talmud. Rabbi Schulweis is an inventor of synagogue programs. Among the things he developed are _havurot_ (small groups of families studying and celebrating together) and programs for special needs students.

jewish foundation for the righteous

Rabbi Schulweis is also a founder of major organizations. He is the founding chairman of the **Jewish Foundation for the Righteous**, which fulfills the traditional Jewish value of _hakarat-hatov_, "the searching out and honoring of goodness." It provides assistance to more than 1,200 aged and needy Christians who risked their lives to save Jews during the Holocaust. It also educates teachers and students about the history of the Holocaust and rescue.

jewish world watch

When he learned about the genocide in Darfur, Sudan, Rabbi Schulweis remembered the Holocaust and many post-Holocaust genocides. He gave a sermon to his congregation. Janice Kamenir-Reznik was in the congregation and heard that sermon. Together, Janice and Rabbi Schulweis founded **Jewish World Watch** (JWW) to raise moral consciousness within the synagogue community. The theme of that sermon was "Never Again," and the central idea of Jewish World Watch is "Do Not Stand Idly By." It is a Jewish response to horrors done by human beings against others.

Based upon the basic lessons of the Torah, JWW works to combat and prevent genocide worldwide—beginning with the genocide in Darfur. It has also recently decided to address the ongoing conflict in the Democratic Republic of Congo. JWW combats and prevents genocide through three main strategies: **education** to raise awareness in the community about ongoing genocide and mass atrocities, **advocacy** on the local, national and international levels in support of policies that will help end genocide, and **refugee relief** projects that provide both desperately needed aid and opportunities for development to the survivors of genocide.

These three efforts together help to build a community of people in the US ready to sound the alarm on genocide wherever and whenever it occurs. Some of the strongest members of this community are young people, who have the enthusiasm and energy to make great change. Young people throughout Los Angeles have joined JWW's ACT program—its Activist Certification and Training program. Through this program, young people create clubs and together work to educate, advocate, and raise funds for refugee relief projects. After finishing three projects (one in each theme), students earn their certification as official JWW Youth Activists—and have earned the skills they need to take action on any issue, anytime.

darfur

Darfur is the western region of Sudan in Africa. During the current conflict there, hundreds of thousands of people have been killed and millions more pushed out of their homes.

The world knows about the Darfur genocide, but the horror continues. There are an estimated 400,000 civilians dead and three million refugees. There have been mass attacks of women and starvation among the entire population.

your tikkun olam organization

Imagine you could be like Janice Kamenir Reznick and Rabbi Harold Schulweis and start your own *tikkun olam* organization.

1. What problem would your organization work on?

2. What would your organization do?

3. What would you call the organization?

janice kamenir-reznik

Janice has long cared about *tikkun olam*. She has a double degree in social work and Jewish communal service and served as the director of the Commission on Soviet Jewry for the Los Angeles Jewish Federation. Then she attended law school and practiced environmental real estate law. During those years in practice Janice was an active volunteer in many *tikkun olam* activities.

In 2002 Janice retired from practicing to work full-time as a volunteer. She wasn't sure where Darfur was on the map when she heard a Rosh ha-Shanah sermon by Rabbi Schulweis. But that soon changed. She joined with him in creating **Jewish World Watch**. She is the founding President. She has helped to mobilize the Jewish community, especially young students, to turn knowledge about Darfur into *tikkun olam*.

tikkun olam text: globalism and judaism

Here is a small piece of the sermon given by Rabbi Schulweis when he called for the creation of **Jewish World Watch**. It is the sermon that was heard by Janice Kamenir-Reznik.

I say: "Never again!" Was this vow only to protect Jews from genocide? I remember what you and I said..."Where are the nations of the world? Where are the churches of the world? Where are the priests, pastors, the bishops and the Pope?"

And will my children and grandchildren ask of me, "And where was the synagogue, where were the rabbis, and where were you during Rwanda, when genocide took place in 1994?"...

Can I shut the newspapers? Do I dare shut my eyes and my ears so as not to see, not to hear, what is going on in God's world? You and I know that the real question is not "Why does God not intervene?" The question is "Why do God's partners, in whose nostrils God breathed Divine potentiality, pretend that they are mute, paralyzed, deaf, powerless?"...

"Few are guilty," my teacher Heschel wrote, "but all are responsible." We are responsible to protect each other, to love and protect the stranger, the pariah, the weak, those of another color, those of another faith. We need to cry out to the world and to influence the world, beginning with ourselves, to tell them, "Lay not your hands upon the innocent. Do not do anything to harm them, for they are God's children."

Harold M. Schulweis
Rosh ha-Shanah, 2004

1. To what do the words "never again" usually refer?
2. How does Rabbi Schulweis apply their meaning?
3. How does he explain the question "Why does God allow genocide in Darfur?" With what question does he replace it?
4. What is the meaning of Heschel's teaching, "Few are guilty but all are responsible"?
5. What does this sermon teach about *tikkun olam*?

solar cooker

Jewish World Watch is doing a simple thing to solve a big problem. They are providing solar cookers in the refugee camps. In this way women are not at risk of attack because they don't have to leave the protection of the camp to search for wood. These cookers make a big difference. A simple act can be help repair the world. To help them: http://www.jewishworldwatch.org/donate/solarcookerproject.html.

tikkun olam activity: tikkun olam and good deeds

Tikkun olam is about fixing the brokenness in the world. It is about helping to redeem the world. Redemption is when the world is transformed into the kind of place that God wanted to create. God gave us a lot of *mitzvot*. Many of them make us better people. Many of them make us better Jews. Not all of them seem to repair the world.

For discussion (and there are no right answers): Which of the following are acts of *tikkun olam*, and which are just good deeds? To prepare for the discussion, check off the ones you think are acts of *tikkun olam*.

_____ Giving food to a food shelter

_____ Helping your sister with homework

_____ Going to a concert for disaster relief

_____ Playing for free at a concert for disaster relief

_____ Admitting a mistake

_____ Working at a synagogue picnic

_____ Building a house for a homeless person

_____ Giving money to a symphony orchestra

_____ Supporting Israel

_____ Working for a political candidate

_____ Donating used clothes to a charity thrift shop

_____ Carrying groceries from the car to your house

_____ Raising money to help protect the rainforests

_____ Putting fifty cents in a donation box

_____ Avoiding a fight with a friend

_____ Using a bicycle rather than a car

shmirat ha-teva

Shmirat ha-Teva means "guarding the environment." Even though you won't find the words *Shmirat ha-Teva* in the Bible or in the Talmud, you will find these ideas.

Shmitah (the Sabbatical year) is a biblical rule that the land must be allowed to rest every seven years. Nothing can be planted or harvested.

Tu b'Shevat (the fifteenth of the month of Shevat) is the New Year for trees. It is a day that celebrates all things that grow in the ground.

Ba'al Tash'hit (Do not waste or destroy) is a biblical mitzvah that begins by teaching that when you are fighting a war you cannot cut down fruit trees to try to starve your enemy. It turns into a law that says "It is wrong to waste or destroy anything that is useful."

The words *Shmirat ha-Teva* come from an Israeli organization. In 1953 a group of Israelis started The Society for the Protection of Nature in Israel, one of the world's oldest ecological organizations. It is dedicated to guarding Israel's open spaces, protecting its coasts and beaches and promoting sustainable development in order to protect the country's natural resources for future generations.

Shmirat ha-Teva means that it is our responsibility to protect the environment not only in Israel but all over the world.

11

shmirat ha-teva text: the tree

A man was journeying in the desert. He was hungry, tired and thirsty. He found a tree with sweet fruits, good shade and a stream of water running under it. He ate its fruits, drank the water and rested in its shade. When he was ready to continue his journey, he said, "Tree, with what shall I bless you? What shall I say to you? 'May your fruits be sweet'? They are already sweet! 'May you provide good shade'? You already provide good shade! 'May a stream of water flow under you'? A stream of water already flows under you! Therefore I will say, 'May it be God's will that all the seedlings taken from you be like you.'"

Ta'anit 5b-6a

1. What lesson can you draw from this story?
2. What does it teach us about *Shmirat ha-Teva*?
3. In the story the man asks God to bless the tree. How can we help God with this blessing?

shmirat ha-teva hero: david ben-gurion

David Ben-Gurion was born in Poland. He became the first prime minister of Israel. In 1906 he was inspired by the Zionist dream and moved to Palestine.

israeli leader

During the time of the Holocaust, 1936 to 1947, while millions of Jews were rounded up and murdered by the Germans, Ben-Gurion worked in two different directions. On one hand he got tens of thousands of young Jews from Palestine to join the British army to fight the Nazis. At the same time he created an underground agency to sneak past the British (who ruled Eretz Yisrael) and illegally bring Jewish refugees from Europe into Palestine.

On May 14, 1948, in accordance with a U.N. resolution, Ben-Gurion proclaimed Israel's independence. He became the first prime minister of Israel.

the negev

The Negev is the southern sixty percent of the state of Israel. It is a beautiful, difficult, stony desert. While Abraham spent time in the Negev and kings David and Solomon had copper mines there, it was never a place where many people lived. When Ben-Gurion was founding the state of Israel the people in the Negev were primarily Beduoins who wandered with their flocks from place to place.

Ben-Gurion believed two things about the Negev. First, it was a good place for Jews to settle because it was wide open and few people lived there. Second, he believed that the Jewish people would become stronger if they made the desert bloom. He set a personal example by choosing to settle in a kibbutz at the center of the Negev. Ben-Gurion worked to establish the National Water Carrier, a huge engineering project to bring water to the area.

his later years

In 1953, David Ben-Gurion was exhausted by years of public service, and he resigned from the government. He settled in Kibbutz Sde Boker. In 1955 he returned to politics. Finally, in June 1970, Ben-Gurion retired forever and returned to Sde Boker. He was known for writing a great deal, for having a unique philosophical outlook, for being an activist and an optimist, for being stubborn and for being an old man who cared about physical fitness. Because of the fitness commitment he stood on his head a lot. Ben-Gurion died in 1973.

While Ben-Gurion's public life was devoted to the political challenges that faced Israel, his private life was lived in the desert. He was really concerned with *shmirat ha-teva* and with working with the environment to turn the desert into a place where people could live.

David Ben-Gurion said these things about the Negev:

"The Negev is one of the Jewish nation's safe places."

"It is in the Negev that the creativity and pioneering energy of Israel will be tested."

"The desert gives us the best opportunity to begin again... When I looked out my window today and saw a tree standing before me, the sight awoke in me a greater sense of beauty and personal satisfaction than all the forests that I have crossed in Switzerland and Scandinavia. For we planted each tree in this place and watered them with the water we provided through much effort. Why does a mother love her children so? Because they are her creation... The trees at Sde Boker speak to me differently than do the trees planted elsewhere. Not only because I participated in their planting and in their maintenance, but also because they are a person's gift to nature."

1. For Ben-Gurion, what makes a tree at Sde Boker different from other trees?

2. How does the desert give us the chance to start over? What is special about the desert?

3. How was *shmirat ha-teva* a big value in Ben-Gurion's life?

in the negev

Ben-Gurion's dream of making the Negev bloom is coming true in Israel today. The Negev is a major center for ecological experimentation. Among the things they are working on are:

BRACKISH WATER: Brackish water is water that has a salt content that is not as high as the ocean, but that is much higher than ordinary groundwater. Farmers in the Negev are growing organic and specialty crops such as cherry tomatoes, melons, peppers, wine grapes, olives, pomegranates, jojoba (used in cosmetics), and strawberries, all irrigated with brackish water.

DESALINATION: Desalination is taking the salt and minerals out of sea water and turning it into fresh water. Israel is one of the world's leaders in this technology. The world's biggest desalination plant is in Ashkelon, and much of its water is used in the Negev.

OLIVE ORCHARDS: Olive trees require minimal irrigation, so they are a great crop for cultivation in the Negev.

GROWING IN SAND DUNES: Large quantities of sand were trucked into the Negev. Now there is huge success with sand used instead of soil for plant cultivation.

AQUACULTURE: Aquaculture is the commercial farming of marine animals. The farming of fish is growing in the Negev.

a new kind of kibbutz grows

An old Zionist song goes "We came to the land to build it and to be built by it." In many ways that is the story of Kibbutz Lotan. The kibbutz is looking to "greenly" make the desert green. The kibbutz has only four cars for one hundred people!

Kibbutz Lotan was established in 1983 by graduates of the Reform Jewish youth movements from Israel and overseas. They came together to create a community based on a modern liberal approach to Jewish values. Lotan's population is evenly divided between native-born Israelis and immigrants from all over the world.

Lotan is in the Arava Desert in the south of Israel. They are far away from cities in a quiet area in beautiful desert surroundings. Their green economy is based on date plantations, dairy, tourism, a holistic health center, field crops and aquaculture. In 1995, a few dedicated members began pushing for a greater emphasis on environmental concerns and ecology.

a green kibbutz

Lotan's Center for Creative Ecology is rooted in *tikkun olam*. The center started with a small desert organic garden and expanded to include an ecological theme park, a migratory bird reserve and nature trails. It now includes alternative building construction within the kibbutz and in the region. It has an unique desert ecological education center that combines hands-on, experiential environmental education in creative recycling, organic gardening and alternative building techniques.

Highlights at the center include Noah's Ark, a playground built of used tires, garbage, and local earth; Captain Compost and His Compost Educational Corner, with splendid organic vegetable gardens and orchards; and The Living Dome, a geodesic dome covered in vines where guests are served organic herbal tea cooked in a solar oven.

The community also features green buildings (mostly of mud and straw with abundant use of trash) bottles, cans and tires as building materials. There is graywater recycling (reusing water used once already) and permaculture gardening (gardening that preserves rather than diminishes the environment).

Kibbutz Lotan lives *Shmirat ha-Teva*. This is Ben-Gurion's dream come true.

kibbutz life

Imagine that you could start your own small settlement in the wilderness. What would be some of your big commitments?

1. _____

2. _____

3. _____

4. _____

5. _____

shmirat ha-teva activity

Circle seven of the ideas below that you think that your family could do that would make a big impact on the environment. Then try to do them.

1. Recycle newspaper, aluminum, glass, plastic and tin
2. Reuse, recycle or return egg cartons and grocery bags
3. Use rags instead of paper towels
4. Use the back of discardable paper for scratch paper
5. Be responsible and creative with leftover food
6. Mend and repair rather than discard and replace
7. Buy organic, pesticide/antibiotic-free foods
8. Grow your own food (in even a small kitchen garden)
9. Volunteer to start or help with a community garden
10. Compost food scraps; give meat scraps to animals
11. Eat foods low on the food chain, not meat
12. Buy locally grown produce and other foods
13. Plant trees in you community
14. Plant plants that require less maintenance and water in your yard
15. Install a water-conserving shower head
16. Turn off the water while you brush your teeth
17. Be sure your home is well insulated
18. Turn off lights when they are not in use
19. In cold weather, lower your thermostat and wear warm clothes

20. Take shorter showers
21. Conserve gas by walking, bicycling, carpooling and riding the bus
22. Use rechargeable batteries; recycle old batteries
23. Exercise regularly and eat nutritious foods
24. Collect the water you run to heat up the water for a bath or shower to use to wash dishes or water plants, or for other purposes
25. Tell others about creative things you have done to be green
26. Grow three herbs
27. Go to a farmers' market
28. Use cloth bags at the grocery store
29. Check tire pressure on the car (properly filled tires use less gas)
30. Donate to a green cause
31. Have an energy audit done on your home
32. Research a vegetarian diet's impact on the planet
33. Use public transportation
34. Find environmentally friendly dry cleaners
35. Turn off or unplug electronic and computer equipment when not in use
36. Replace incandescent bulbs with compact fluorescent lamps (CFLs)

shmirat ha-guf

Shmirat ha-guf means "guarding the body". It is the *mitzvah* to treat your body as a holy place. In the Torah we are told: "TAKE CARE OF YOURSELF, AND GUARD YOUR SOUL DILIGENTLY" (Deuteronomy 4:9). Rabbi Naḥman of Bratzlav taught, "Every person must take great care of his or her physical body" (*Likutei Moharan* I, 22:5).

Rabbi Elliot Dorff wrote, "American law would permit me to eat a half-gallon of ice cream every night of the week. I might be stupid to do so because I will look and feel terrible and endanger my life, but that is my choice. In Jewish law, though, I do not have that right because I have a legal duty to take care of my body, since it belongs to God."

Our bodies are holy, and how we use them is a sacred choice. *Shmirat ha-guf* is not just about working out. It is also about drugs, drinking, health care, and a lot of other big issues. Guarding our body has to do with many different things we have to do or not do.

17

shmirat ha-guf text: in the image of god

Once when Hillel had finished a lesson with his students, he started walking with them.

"Master," they asked, "where are you going?"

"To perform a *mitzvah*," he answered.

"Which *mitzvah*?" they asked.

"To take a bath," he answered.

"Is that a *mitzvah*?"

"Yes! A person is appointed to scour and wash the statues of the king that stand in the theaters and stadiums. That person is paid for the work and is even connected with royalty. Since that is so, how much more should I, who am created in the image of God, wash and scrub myself? As it is written, 'IN THE IMAGE OF GOD DID GOD MAKE HUMANKIND' (Genesis 9:6).

(Leviticus Rabbah 34:3)

1. Why is bathing a *mitzvah*?
2. What biblical verse does Hillel use to prove that bathing is a *mitzvah*?
3. Do people look like God? (Isn't God invisible?)
4. How can God's image be a reason to take care of our bodies?

the maccabiah games

The Maccabiah games can't be a hero, but they can be a place where heroes emerge. The Maccabiah Games are the Jewish Olympics. They are held in Israel every four years in the year following the Olympic Games. The best Jewish athletes from throughout the world compete. Israeli Arabs are allowed to compete, too.

The Maccabiah is organized by the Maccabi World Union (MWU). It is a worldwide organization devoted not only to sports but to furthering Jewish identity and traditions. The MWU is headquartered in Israel.

yosef yekutieli

The Maccabiah Games were the brainchild of fifteen-year-old Russian-born Yosef Yekutieli. Yekutieli, who was living in Israel before it was a state, was so excited by the 1912 Olympic Games that he dreamed of a worldwide Jewish Olympics. Even though he was laughed at, he spent the next ten years developing his plan.

In 1928 Yekutieli presented his proposal to the Jewish National Fund. He had the idea that the Maccabiah Games be organized to remember the 1,800th anniversary of the Bar Kochba Rebellion (a Jewish revolt against the Romans). Yekutieli's Maccabiada (as the games were originally called) was the right idea at the right time. The *Eretz Yisrael* Soccer Association and other Holy Land sports groups signed on and gave the proposed games their blessings. Sir Arthur "Andy" Wauchope, British High Commissioner of Palestine, admired the achievements of Zionists in Palestine, including the growing Jewish sports movement. The new High Commissioner gladly supported the Maccabiada on condition that it host Arab and official British Mandate athletes as well as Jewish sportsmen. The Maccabiada was scheduled for March 1932.

marketing the games

The next problem was reaching the world Jewish community. Two delegations of Jewish motor-bikers set off from Tel Aviv on a huge promotional tour to the Jewish communities of Europe, where most Jews lived. The first group of promoters hit the road in 1930, biking from Tel Aviv to Antwerp, Belgium. The second set of riders left Tel Aviv a year later for London. Yekutieli himself rode with one of the delegations.

a success

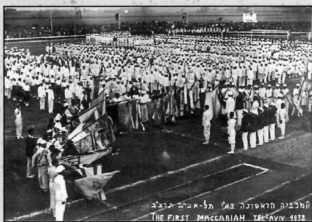

המכבבה הראשונה בא"י תל-אב"ב ב'ארצ'ב
THE FIRST MACCABIAH TEL-AVIV 1932

The original Maccabiah was held March 28 to April 6, 1932. Four hundred athletes competed. Planned to occur every four years, Maccabiah II was moved up a year to 1935 because of the rising tide of Nazism in Europe. World War II forced postponement of the third Maccabiah. The Games today are organized by an International Maccabiah Committee and are sanctioned by the International Olympic Committee and World Federation of Sports. The Maccabiah Games rank among the five largest sports events in the world. Yosef Yekutieli's dream became a *shmirat ha-guf* reality.

To find out how to compete in the American Maccabiah Games or to become part of the American team, check out http://www.maccabiusa.com.

It is ironic that the Maccabees would be the inspiration two thousand years later for a Jewish sports movement. The Maccabean revolt was started by the creation of a gymnasium in Jerusalem by the High Priest Jason. This gym served as a focal point of Greek culture in the heart of the Jewish capital. It was there that Greek-wanna-be Jews, including some of the younger priests, took part in nude athletic contests and the pagan rituals that were part of the Greek sport experience. This angered the Jews who had resisted the ways of their idol-worshipping neighbors for over a thousand years. Among the outraged was the priest Mattathias, who took Judah and his other sons away from Jerusalem to his native Modi'in, where they could live as Jews. When the Maccabees recaptured Jerusalem, one of the first things they did was destroy the gymnasium.

So why the connection between the Maccabees and Jewish sports? It was the heroic quality of the Maccabean struggle that spoke to those who use their name for modern Jewish athletics. The modern Jewish sports movement, and the Maccabi organization that emerged, served to instill a sense of national pride and purpose through sport, playing an important role in facing the dual threats of anti-Semitism and assimilation.

Center for Sport and Jewish Life (http://www.csjl.org/articlereader.php?item=1)

1. What does "ironic" mean?
2. Why would the original Maccabees hate the Maccabiah games?
3. Why did Jewish athletes choose the Maccabees as their role model?
4. What is good about the modern Maccabiah Games?
5. How is this "ironic"?

shmirat ha-guf hero: lenny krayzelburg

from soviet training program to the jcc

Lenny was born in Odessa, Russia in 1975. He was part of the Soviet Union's Olympic training program. At nine years old he was practicing five hours a day. His parents, Oleg and Yelena, were concerned about their son's future. They felt his chances for success would be greater in America. He and his family left the Soviet Union in 1989.

Lenny said, "As a Jew growing up in Russia, I never faced much anti-Semitism. A few times I was called names. But my parents knew that because I was a Jew, my opportunities would be limited there—in sports especially."

In America, Krayzelburg found an aquatic home at the Westside Jewish Community Center in Los Angeles. Two weeks after he arrived in the United States he was back in the water.

hard times

The Krayzelburg family suffered from financial difficulties. Lenny had to travel forty-five minutes each way to swimming practice and didn't get home before 9:30. He had to study English rapidly in order to understand his coaches' instructions. Aided by the Russian Jewish community, he managed to adapt quickly.

At fourteen, when the JCC could not provide him with the challenges he needed, Lenny was tempted to give it all up, but his father talked him out of it.

success, success, and more success

Lenny went to Santa Monica College, where he won both the 100- and 200-yard backstroke junior college titles. On recommendation from his coach, Lenny transferred to U.S.C. and in 1995 became a naturalized citizen. In August of 1999 he broke three world records and won three gold medals at the Pan American Pacific Championships. At the Sydney Olympics Krayzelburg won the gold in the 100-meter backstroke, the 200-meter backstroke and the 400-meter medley relay, breaking two Olympic records in the process. In 2004 he finished second in the American trials and secured a place in the Athens Olympics. He missed out on a medal by just .02 second. Krayzelburg made up for this by helping the American team to win yet another Olympic gold in the 4 x 100m relay.

a jewish athelete

Being Jewish, Krayzelburg wanted to take the once-in-a-lifetime chance to compete with other top Jewish athletes at the 2001 Maccabiah Games in Israel. It was his childhood dream to visit Israel. He was selected to carry the flag for the United States team. He earned a gold medal and set a new Maccabiah record in the 100-meter backstroke. He also won a gold medal in the 4 x 100m medley relay.

While Krayzelburg has had no Jewish education and celebrates only the holiday of Yom Kippur by going to synagogue, he is interested in his Jewish roots. "Being Jewish is a part of me. It's a part of my culture. I find it fascinating, and I want to learn as much about it as possible. I hope to raise my own children with more religion. I hope to sometime become involved in charitable causes in the Jewish community."

and some say teach them to swim

In July 2005 Lenny opened swimming schools operating out of the JCC (Jewish Community Center) system. Lenny lives *shmirat ha-guf* and helps others to do so.

This is an excerpt from Lenny Krayzelburg's blogs.

May 24th, 2007

On a personal level I feel that I had an amazing career that included four Olympic gold medals. What I feel most proud of is the fact that I accomplished all of my success without even taking simple vitamins. If you look at hundreds of drug test forms that I had to fill out throughout my career, there was always a line across the space that was allocated to list medications and supplements that the athlete is taking.

I know deep in my heart that there are swimmers and athletes in general that value integrity and respect for the history of their sport and compete clean with clear consciences.

Lenny

http://www.swimroom.com

1. Why does Lenny make a big deal out of not taking dietary supplements?
2. What does this blog entry teach about *shmirat ha-guf*?
3. When is the best body not the best image of God?

lenny's other mitzvah

Here is a passage from the Talmud that talks about adults' obligations to children:

These are the obligations which a father is to do for his son... The father is bound in respect to his son: to circumcise, redeem (a ceremony called *pidyon ha-ben*), teach him Torah, take a wife for him and teach him a craft. Some say to teach him to swim, too.

(Kiddushin 29a)

1. All (or almost all) of the other obligations are Jewish events. Why is teaching a child to swim on the list?
2. How does Lenny help parents fulfill the "teach them to swim" mitzvah?

rodef shalom

A *rodef shalom* is someone who chases after peace. In the book of Psalms (34:15) it says: "SEEK PEACE AND CHASE IT." This verse is explained in the midrash. "Rabbi Yohanan explained the text teaches that to have peace one should be like a captain on a boat. 'A person should always be on the lookout for an opportunity and then pursue a course towards peace.'" *(Leviticus Rabbah. 21:5)*

The Jewish tradition teaches that peacemaking is a way of life. It has to do with the way we treat other people every day. Here is one description of a person who is a *rodef shalom*. "A peace-loving person is by no means a weakling or a coward. He is prepared to speak out against injustice, indeed, to become angry when encountering evil in others. But even in his anger, he looks upon his opponent as a potential friend who will eventually change his ways and appreciate the effort that is being made to help him." (Simon Glustrom, *The Language of Judaism*)

Judaism believes that a person should be a *rodef shalom*, someone who does more than avoid fighting—someone who actively pursues peace.

23

rodef shalom text: aaron's story

"SEEK PEACE AND CHASE IT." (Psalms 34:15)

Hillel used to say: "Be one of the disciples of Aaron, loving peace and chasing peace, be one who loves others and brings them close to Torah." (*Pirkei Avot* 1:12)

Whenever Aaron heard that two people were involved in an argument or quarrel he would go to one of them and tell him that he had recently met his friend and heard him say, "The fight was my fault. I am really sorry it happened." Aaron would then go to the second person and tell him the same made-up story. When the two would meet again they would hug and be friends. This is why the entire nation cried when Aaron died. (*Avot de Rabbi Natan* 12:3 on Numbers 20:29)

1. What is the difference between "seeking peace" and "chasing peace"?
2. How was Aaron a *rodef shalom*?
3. What are ways you can be a *rodef shalom*?

rodef shalom hero: yitzhak rabin

child of zionists

Yitzhak Rabin was born in Jerusalem in March 1922. His father immigrated to Israel from the United States, and he served in World War I as a volunteer in the Jewish Legion. His mother, Rosa, was one of the first members of the Haganah, the Jewish defense organization.

military career

After completing his schooling at Kadoorie Agricultural High School, Rabin volunteered for the Palmah, the commando unit of the Jewish community. He served in the Palmah and the Israeli army for twenty-seven years, becoming IDF (Israeli Defense Forces) Chief of Staff. Retiring from the army in 1968, he was appointed Israeli ambassador to the United States.

life in politics

Rabin returned to Jerusalem in 1973 and became active in the Israel Labor Party. In the December elections he was elected to the Knesset and he became minister of labor. In 1974 Rabin became prime minister.

As prime minister Rabin placed an emphasis on improving the economy, solving social problems and strengthening the IDF. Following the Labor Party's defeat in 1977, Rabin served as a member of Knesset. In 1984 he served as minister of defense.

rodef shalom

In 1992 he was elected prime minister again. For many years Israel had been in conflict with the Palestinians, a group of Arabs who lived in Eretz Yisrael before the state of Israel was established. On September 13, 1993, after working with President Clinton, Rabin and PLO (Palestinian Liberation Organization) Chairman Yasir Arafat signed the Declaration of Principles in Washington, D.C. This document outlined a peace agreement between Israel and the PLO and said that Israel would work with the Palestinians to establish their own government.

After a famous picture shaking hands with Arafat, Rabin commented that one has to make peace with one's enemies, not

with one's friends. Rabin received the 1994 Nobel Peace Prize together with Israeli Foreign Minister Shimon Peres and Chairman Arafat. He began negotiations with the Palestinians on self-rule in Gaza and some areas of the West Bank and on the creation of a Palestinian authority. In October of that year Rabin and King Hussein of Jordan signed the Israel–Jordan peace treaty.

On November 4, 1995, Yitzhak Rabin was assassinated by a Israeli who was against the peace process. Rabin was attending a mass rally for peace with the slogan "Yes to Peace, No to Violence." Prime Minister Rabin was laid to rest on Mount Herzl in Jerusalem. His funeral was attended by many world leaders, among them U.S. president Bill Clinton, Egyptian president Hosni Mubarak and King Hussein of Jordan. Bill Clinton delivered a eulogy whose memorable final words were in Hebrew: "*Shalom haver* (Goodbye, friend)."

Rabin was both a warrior and a *rodef shalom*. While much of his life was devoted to creating and defending the State of Israel, he also worked hard to bring peace between Israel and her neighbors.

rodef shalom text: accepting the nobel prize

Here is a small part of the speech Yitzhak Rabin gave when he accepted the Nobel Peace Prize.

Ladies and Gentlemen,

The profession of soldiering embraces a certain paradox. We take the best and the bravest of our young men into the army. We supply them with equipment which costs a virtual fortune. We rigorously train them for the day when they must do their duty—and we expect them to do it well. Yet we fervently pray that that day will never come—that the planes will never take off, the tanks will never move forward, the soldiers will never mount the attacks for which they have been trained so well.

We pray that it will never happen, because of the sanctity of life...

In the coming days, a special commission of the Israel Defense Forces will finish drafting a Code of Conduct for our soldiers. The formulation regarding human life will read as follows, and I quote: "In recognition of its supreme importance, the soldier will preserve human life in every way possible and endanger himself, or others, only to the extent deemed necessary to fulfill this mission..."

For many years ahead—even if wars come to an end, after peace comes to our land—these words will remain a pillar of fire which goes before our camp, a guiding light for our people. And we take pride in that.

1. What is a paradox?
2. What does Rabin mean by "the sanctity of life"?
3. What does this speech tell us about Rabin's commitment to be a *rodef shalom*?

rodef shalom in a small way

A *rodef shalom* can be like Yitzhak Rabin and help to make peace between nations. He or she can also be like Aaron and make peace between neighbors. What are three things you can do to make peace in your community?

1. _____

2. _____

3. _____

rodef shalom heroes: the four chaplains

This is a story about *kiddush ha-Shem* (martyrdom) and *pikuah nefesh* (saving a life), but it is also a story about *rodef shalom* because of the way the four chaplains worked together.

the dorchester

It was World War II and Germany was fighting the United States and a group of other countries called the allies. Lots of American soldiers were being sent in ships across the Atlantic Ocean in order to be able to fight. Germany was attacking US ships with their submarines and so it was dangerous to sail across the Atlantic. On February 2, 1943 the U.S.S. Dorchester was crowded with 902 men. It was heading toward an American base in Greenland. The captain ordered the men to sleep in their clothing and keep life jackets on (in case the ship was attacked). Many soldiers sleeping in the bottom of the ship didn't obey the order because of the heat from the engine. Others ignored it because life jackets were uncomfortable.

the attack

A German submarine approached on the surface. Three torpedoes were fired. One hit was deadly. It hit the ship far below the water line.

When the captain was told that his ship was sinking, he gave the order to abandon ship. It took less than twenty minutes for the Dorchester to sink. The blast from the torpedo had killed many men, and many more were seriously wounded. Others were lost in the darkness. Men jumped from the ship into lifeboats, overcrowding them to the point of capsizing. Other rafts, tossed into the Atlantic, drifted away before soldiers could get in them.

the chaplains

This is the story of the four chaplains. A chaplain is a religious leader like a rabbi or minister who joins the army to serve the religious needs of soldiers.

The chaplains were Lieutenant George L. Fox (Protestant), Lieutenant Alexander D. Goode (Jewish); Lieutenant John P. Washington, (Catholic) and Lieutenant Clark V. Poling, (Protestant). The worked hard to bring hope in this darkness. They spread out among the soldiers and tried to calm the frightened, help the wounded and guide the confused toward safety.

One witness, Private William B. Bednar, was floating in the water surrounded by dead bodies and debris. He said, "I could hear men crying, pleading, praying. I could also hear the chaplains preaching courage. Their voices were the only thing that kept me going."

Another sailor, Petty Officer John J. Mahoney, tried to go back to his cabin, but Rabbi Goode stopped him. Mahoney, scared of the cold Arctic air, was going back for his gloves. "Never mind," Goode told him. "I have two pairs." The rabbi gave Mahoney his own gloves. Later Mahoney realized that Rabbi Goode was not carrying two pairs of gloves. He realized that the rabbi had decided not to leave the Dorchester.

When there were no more lifejackets in the storage room, the chaplains removed theirs and gave them to four frightened young men. "It was the finest thing I have seen or hope to see this side of heaven," said John Ladd, another survivor.

an act of rodef shalom

As the ship went down, survivors in nearby rafts could see the four chaplains—arms linked and braced against the slanting deck. Their voices could also be heard offering prayers. Of the 902 men aboard the Dorchester, only 230 survived.

By working together the four chaplains taught that religion doesn't have to divide people. They showed that all people were created by one God. The memory of their shared bravery is an example of *rodef shalom*, of people working together for a better future.

rodef shalom activity: mission statement of the four chaplains memorial foundation

The Four Chaplains Memorial Foundation was dedicated on February 3, 1951, by President Harry S. Truman. In his dedication speech the president said, "This interfaith shrine... will stand through long generations to teach Americans that as men can die heroically as brothers so should they live together in mutual faith and goodwill." This is the foundation's mission statement:

THE FOUR CHAPLAINS MEMORIAL FOUNTAIN

The Four Chaplains Memorial Foundation exists to further the cause of "unity without uniformity" by encouraging goodwill and cooperation among all people. The organization achieves its mission honoring people whose deeds symbolize the legacy of the Four Chaplains. The Four Chaplains Memorial Foundation's vision is to impart the principles of selfless service to humanity without regard to race, creed, ethnicity or religious belief.

1. What does "unity with uniformity" mean?
2. What is the mission of this foundation?
3. How does it help to create people who are *rodfei shalom?*

zikaron

value: zikaron

The three Hebrew letters זכר form a root that has to do with memory: remembering. Jews are big on remembering. Just about every Jewish holiday tells the story of some major past event. We light a candle and say *Kaddish* on the anniversary of someone's death. And on the three festivals and at Yom Kippur we say *Yizkor* (remembering prayers) for those who have died.

Yom ha-Zikaron is the day before *Yom ha-Aztmaut*, Israeli Independence Day. The fourth of *Iyyar* is a day devoted to remembering soldiers killed defending the state of Israel. Many Israelis go to the cemetery. At the end of the day, after two minutes of silence, sirens are sounded. A new holiday is begun. It is a day of parades and dancing in the street. It is the celebration of the State of Israel.

Zikaron also has to do with the Holocaust. *Yom ha-Shoah* is **Holocaust Remembrance Day.** It is observed as a day of commemoration of the approximately six million Jews who perished in the Holocaust. In Israel it is a national memorial day. In other counties it is observed by Jews in synagogues and communities.

The Hebrew word *yad* (hand) also means "memorial". The national Holocaust Martyrs and Heroes Remembrance Authority in Israel is called *Yad Vashem* because Isaiah 56:5 says: "AND TO THEM WILL I GIVE IN MY HOUSE AND WITHIN MY WALLS *A MEMORIAL AND A NAME* (*Yad va-Shem)* THAT SHALL NOT BE CUT OFF."

This is the text of the *Erev Shabbat* (Friday night) *Kiddush*. It teaches us a big lesson about *zikaron*.

Blessed be You, the Eternal
our God, Ruler-of-the-Cosmos,
the One-Who-creates the fruit of the vine.
Blessed are You, the Eternal
our God, Ruler-of-the-Cosmos,
The One-Who-made-us-holy through the *mitzvot*
and One-Who-is-pleased with us
and the One-Who-gave us the holy Shabbat
with love and satisfaction
as a *zikaron* (remembrance) of the work of creation.
Because this is a day of Halellujah
A holy time
Zekher (remembering) the exodus from Egypt.
Because you chose us and separated us from other peoples
and intentionally separated Shabbat with love
as our inheritance,
Blessed be You, Eternal,
the One-Who-makes Shabbat holy.

1. The *Kiddush* teaches us that Shabbat is about remembering two moments in history. What are they?

2. Almost every Jewish holiday remembers a moment in history. What moment does each of these holidays remember?

   a. Passover

   b. Shavuot

   c. Sukkot

   d. Hanukkah

   e. Purim

zikaron hero: elie wiesel

Elie Wiesel's statement, "...to remain silent and indifferent is the greatest sin of all..." is a perfect outline of his views on life and is at the center of his work. Elie Wiesel is the author of fifty-seven books dealing with Judaism and the Holocaust, the best known of which is *Night*. It is a memoir that describes his experiences during the Holocaust and his imprisonment in several concentration camps.

Paris, France. He taught Hebrew and worked as a choirmaster. Then he became a professional journalist. For ten years after the war Wiesel refused to write about or discuss his experiences during the Holocaust. Eventually Wiesel wrote a short autobiographical manuscript in French, *La Nuit*, which was later translated into English as *Night*.

Night started out as a failure. It sold just 1,046 copies during its first eighteen months. But it attracted interest from reviewers, leading to television interviews with Wiesel. "The first printing was three thousand copies," Wiesel said, "And it took three years to sell them. Now I get a hundred letters a month from children about the book. And there are many, many million copies in print." On January 16, 2006, Oprah Winfrey chose the novel for her book club. One million extra paperback and 150,000 hardcover copies were printed.

childhood

Elie Wiesel was born on September 30, 1928 in a little town called Sighet, Transylvania (in Romania), to Chlomo and Sarah Wiesel. Chlomo was an Orthodox Jew and a shopkeeper who ran a grocery store. It was Chlomo who gave his son a strong sense of humanity, encouraging him to learn modern Hebrew and to read literature. His mother encouraged him to study Torah and Kabbalah.

On May 16, 1944, the Nazis deported the Jewish community of Sighet to Auschwitz-Birkenau. Wiesel was fifteen. While he was at Auschwitz, the number A-7713 was tattooed on his left arm. He was separated from his mother and sister. Wiesel and his father were sent to the attached work camp Buna-Werke. He and his father were forced to work under horrible conditions and moved between concentration camps. Just a few weeks after the two were marched to Buchenwald, Wiesel's father was murdered by the Nazis. It was only months before the camp was liberated.

after the war

After the war Wiesel was placed in a French orphanage, where he was reunited with his older sisters, Hilda and Bea. In 1948 he studied philosophy at the Sorbonne, a famous university in

in the united states

In 1955 Wiesel moved to New York City as a U.S. citizen. He was awarded the Nobel Peace Prize in 1986 for speaking out against violence, repression and racism. Wiesel and his wife Marion started the Elie Wiesel Foundation for Humanity. He served as chairman of the Presidential Commission on the Holocaust, which became the U.S. Holocaust Memorial Council.

Not only is Wiesel one of the most important voices in the *zikaron*, memory, of the Holocaust, but he has turned that memory into advocacy for many causes: Israel, Soviet and Ethiopian Jews, the victims of *apartheid* in South Africa, Argentina's *desaparecidos* (disapeared), Bosnian victims of genocide in the former Yugoslavia, Nicaragua's Miskito Indians and the Kurds. You can add to that list speaking out for victims in Darfur.

Wiesel was awarded the Nobel Peace Prize in 1986. The Nobel Committee called him a "messenger to mankind."

zikaron text: elie wiesel quotation

Here are five texts by Elie Wiesel. Find a partner. Read these texts out loud. Translate each text into your own words and pick your favorite.

[a] That is my major preoccupation, memory, the kingdom of memory. I want to protect and enrich that kingdom, glorify that kingdom and serve it.

[b] I decided to devote my life to telling the story because I felt that having survived I owe something to the dead. And anyone who does not remember betrays them again.

April 16, 1945, Buchenwald, Germany. Slave laborers in the Buchenwald Concentration Camp. Many had died of malnutrition when U.S. troops arrived and entered the camp. Elie Wiesel is the man whose face can be seen on the far right of the center bunk.

© BETTMANN/CORBIS

[c] I marvel at the resilience of the Jewish people. Their best characteristic is their desire to remember. No other people has such an obsession with memory.

[d] I swore never to be silent whenever and wherever human beings endure suffering and humiliation. We must always take sides. Neutrality helps the oppressor, never the victim. Silence encourages the tormentor, never the tormented.

[e] The opposite of love is not hate, it's indifference. The opposite of art is not ugliness, it's indifference. The opposite of faith is not heresy, it's indifference. And the opposite of life is not death, it's indifference.

1. Explain Eli Wiesel's commitment to *zikaron*.
2. Explain how he connects *zikaron* to *tikkun olam*.

being like elie wiesel

You can say, "I am not like Elie Wiesel. I know nothing that should be remembered." But that is not true. Everyone has memories worth passing on. What is one thing you know that should be remembered?

_____

_____

_____

_____

_____

_____

Dov Noy is someone you've probably never heard of, who does something you may not have known that anyone does. Still, he is an important *zikaron* hero. Dov Noy is one of the world's foremost authorities on Jewish folklore. He collects and studies Jewish folk stories and fairy tales.

Dov Noy came to Israel from Poland in 1938. Today he lives in Jerusalem. During World War II he served in the British army. After the war he continued his education at the Hebrew University, Yale, and then Indiana University. In 1956 Dov Noy founded the Haifa Ethnological Museum and Folklore Archives. In 2004 he won the Israel prize.

Folktales are a special piece of history of a people, but they are almost never written down. They are told out loud and passed from generation to generation. Jewish folktales have moved from country to country, continent to continent, language to language as the Jewish people moved around the world. Because the tellers of these tales were ordinary people, not important rabbis or scholars, the stories fell below the radar and were not recorded.

When he was a graduate student at Indiana University Dov studied under Stith Thompson, the founder of the modern study of folklore. Dov Noy realized that large pieces of tradition were being lost. He decided to devote his life to rescuing Jewish folktales before they vanished. The first step he took in accomplishing this mission was to found the Israel Folktale Archives in 1955. He was the founder of the entire field of Jewish folklore and the teacher of every younger Jewish folklore scholar throughout the world. When someone tells you a Jewish story, we probably know it because of the work of Dov Noy. He has collected and cataloged more than 23,000 stories. That, too, is an act of *zikaron*.

zikaron activity: a folktale

The author learned this story from Howard Schwartz, who learned it from Dov Noy.

the bird of happiness

There was a special light that shone when God created the world. It disappeared when Adam and Eve left the Garden. God took a piece of this light, put it in a crystal and gave it to Adam and Eve to light the darkness. The crystal was passed from generation to generation. Noah used this crystal to light the inside of the ark. It was passed from Abraham to Isaac to Jacob and made it to Solomon, who used it to light the inside of the Temple. When the Temple was destroyed it disappeared.

Aaron was a Jewish boy. He and his family were escaped slaves walking through a desert. One night Aaron had a dream of being lost in a sandstorm and being rescued by a large white bird. When he awoke he found a glowing crystal in his hand. He hung it from a leather thong around his neck. It glowed only when they were walking in the right direction. It led them to pools of water and oases filled with fruit. It led them to a great city. They learned that the king had died and the city needed a new one. To find the new king they released the Bird of Happiness. When it landed on Aaron's shoulder, the boy who had been a slave became the new king. It was the bird of his dream.

The people dressed him in robes and put a crown on his head. His family now lived in a palace. The crystal became a guide. It would glow when the right answer was yes. It would remain dark if the right answer was no. One hour a day Aaron sneaked away to a shack. He took off his royal garb and put on the rags he had worn as a slave. He wanted to remember where he had come from. He also gave thanks every day for the blessings that the Bird of Happiness brought.

1. Why did the boy put on his slave clothes every day?

2. How is this a Jewish thing to do?

3. What does this story teach us about the power of *zikaron?*

kol yisrael arevim zeh ba-zeh

value: kol yisrael arevim zeh ba-zeh

The Talmud, teaches, "*Kol Yisrael arevim zeh ba-zeh*—All Israel is responsible one for the other" (*Shavuot 39a*).

This doesn't mean that Jews should care only about other Jews, but that every Jew should recognize that there is a connection between all Jews. Every Jew has an obligation to help another Jew if he or she is in need.

This statement from the Talmud is part of *ahavat Yisrael*, love for Israel. This is an obligation for every Jew. *Ahavat Yisrael* means "love of Israel"—but who is Israel? We don't mean just the country. Israel is all of us. All Jews alive today together make up this massive thing called Israel. And that's why Israel the country is named Israel—because it's the place that is home to Israel—all Jews. So "love of Israel" means love of other Jews.

Kol Yisrael arevim zeh ba-zeh teaches that we have an obligation to support and protect other Jews.

Here is the text from the Talmud where the phrase *Kol Yisrael arevim zeh ba-zeh* is found.

The Torah teaches: "THEY SHALL STUMBLE OVER ONE ANOTHER, AS IF TO ESCAPE A SWORD, THOUGH NO ONE CHASES...." (Leviticus 26:37)

This means that one stumbles because of the sin of the other. This verse teaches us that **all Israel is responsible one for the other.** They are punished (by stumbling) because it was in their power to prevent the sin, and they did not prevent it. (Shavuot 39a)

Rabbi Isaac Luria taught: "This is why the confessional prayer *Al Het* is worded, "For the sin that we have sinned..." All of Israel is one body. Every Jew is part of that body. **All Israel is responsible one for the other.**

1. According to the Talmud, why does one person stumble over another?
2. How does this teach that all Israel is responsible one for the other?
3. What does Rabbi Isaac Luria add to this?
4. What is your understanding of *Kol Yisrael arevim zeh ba-zeh*?

kol yisrael arevim zeh ba-zeh heroes:
robert and myra kraft

meet bob kraft

Robert Kraft was born in Brookline, Massachusetts, on June 5, 1941. He is the son of an Orthodox Jew who wanted him to be a rabbi. Instead he went to Harvard Business School. He married Myra Hiatt, whose father ran Rand-Whitney, a packaging company. Kraft joined the company and bought it in 1972. The same year he started International Forest Products. He owns mills and he manufactures and distributes paper and packaging products in eighty countries. In 1994 Kraft bought the New England Patriots. They won the Super Bowl in 2002, 2004 and 2005.

ahavat yisrael

Kraft has a longstanding love of Israel and its people. Kraft addressed the 2005 graduating class of Columbia College regarding the driving forces in his life: "Family, faith, philanthropy, and *football*." Mr. Kraft termed this combination the "Four Fs."

Robert and Myra have donated tens of millions of dollars to a variety of causes, including education, children's and women's issues, health care, youth sports and Israel. Among the many institutions the Krafts have supported are Columbia University, Harvard Business School, The College of the Holy Cross, Boston College, Tufts University, the Belmont Hill School, the Boys and Girls Clubs of Boston and the Dana Farber Cancer Institute in Boston.

Robert and Myra have donated millions of dollars to all sorts of Israeli charities, including Hadassah Hospital. They helped renovate an after-school program for Ethiopian immigrants. One of their projects is the Kraft Family Stadium in Jerusalem. Built in 2000, it is host to a thirty-three-team flag football league as well as to other sporting events.

visiting israel

The Krafts love to bring groups of people with them to Israel to showcase what they see as the positive aspects of the country. In recent years he has brought Patriots players. Kraft speaks out for Israel: "It is hard for people in America who have never been there, even people who are Jewish, but especially non-Jews, to understand what Israel is about. The way it's represented in the media is sometimes so far from what the truth is. It is such a rich place in terms of history. It's the cradle of all the western religions. So much history has happened."

american football in israel

Israel is a soccer country. When it is not soccer, it is basketball. Still Kraft is funding and creating an American-style football league there. Kraft said, "I just love the sport of football, because it requires intelligence and people pulling together. For me, it is the highest form of competition, which is what makes people great." He also said, "The teamwork in football was a perfect fit for Israel, where we have people from all over the world working together: Russians and Ethiopians, Arabs and Christians."

Robert and Myra Kraft live *tzedakah, tikkun olam*, and *Kol Yisrael aravim zeh ba-zeh.* They take care of the world, take care of the Jewish people and take care of Israel.

kol yisrael arevim zeh ba-zeh activity: the krafts

Myra Kraft, chair of Combined Jewish Philanthropies Board of Directors, gave an interview to *The Boston Globe*. Here are some of the things she said about her connection to Israel.

[1] "My feeling, and Robert's, too, is if you're fortunate enough to have acquired wealth, then it's an obligation on you to give back... This is what I see as my occupation. I don't know how to play bridge, nor do I want to learn how to play bridge. This is what I do."

[2] Myra's first memory of a commitment to help Israel goes back to the Holocaust. In 1948 her father visited the displaced-persons camps of Europe and went to Palestine. And while he was away Myra, then five years old, decided to do something to help. She disappeared before her afternoon kindergarten was scheduled to begin. She says, "I went door to door in my neighborhood, and I asked people to help the poor children in Europe in the displaced-persons camps. My mother got a little frantic until the neighbors started calling. It was just part of the way I grew up, I think."

[3] "I'm not a religious person, and my father wasn't really religious. It's not religion, it's peoplehood. If we don't take care of ourselves, no one is going to take care of us."

1. What do Myra's words teach us about the Krafts as philanthropists?
2. What do Myra's words teach us about them as people who live the value *Kol Yisrael arevim zeh ba-zeh*?

kol yisrael arevim zeh ba-zeh

A Hasidic rabbi taught:

The many letters in the Torah represent the many souls of the Jewish people. If one single letter is left out of the Torah, it is unfit for use. If one single soul is left out of the union of the Jewish people, the Divine Presence will not join them. Like the letters, the souls must join together.

Rabbi Uri of Streslik

1. What is your connection to the Jewish people?
2. What is missing from the Jewish people if you are not there?

kol yisrael arevim zeh ba-zeh hero: rabbi gershom sizomu

Gershom Sizomu from Abayudaya, Uganda (in Africa), is the first black rabbi from sub-Saharan Africa to be ordained by an American rabbinical school. Sizomu was ordained from the Ziegler School of Rabbinic Studies at American Jewish University in Los Angeles with the support of a five-year fellowship from Be'chol Lashon. Gershom, like his father and grandfather before him, is the spiritual leader of the Jewish community in Uganda. He presides over life-cycle ceremonies, conducts religious services and gives the official word in Torah study.

the abayudaya

Less than one hundred years ago, during an effort to convert Ugandans to Christianity, a tribal leader, Semei Kaungulu, was pushed to influence his followers. He was given the Bible to read, and found that the first five books of Moses made more sense to him than the Christian Bible. He became so excited about the teachings of Torah that Kaungulu circumcised himself and began to observe Shabbat and the laws of kashrut. He was followed by eight thousand of his people. After Kaungulu's death in 1928, many members drifted away.

Today Uganda's Jews number over one thousand... they are known as the Abayudaya, which in the Luganda language means "people of Judah."

idi amin

Idi Amin ruled Uganda from 1971 to 1979 and made Judaism illegal. Those who remained Jews became even stronger in their commitment to a life of Torah. Gershom didn't attend synagogue as a young boy. Jews kept observance confined to the home. He remembers, "The only minyan we had was in my father's bedroom...we would ask God to get rid of Idi Amin. Amin was overthrown on erev Pesah, the eleventh of April, 1979. The government declared freedom of worship...the first time I went to synagogue was on the second night of Pesah."

social justice

Today, the Abayudaya Jewish community of Uganda is connecting with Jews around the world to ensure their survival and security. The Abayudaya leadership requested that Be'chol Lashon, an American organization, partner with them to improve healthcare: drill wells for clean water, distribute mosquito nets to combat malaria, and build a health clinic to benefit everybody.

music

Music has long been a motivating force for religion in Africa. It has been critical to the survival of the Abayudaya community. Youth returning to Judaism demanded innovations in the worship service. In addition to the existing music, they resolved to create new melodies accompanied by guitar. Abayudaya community leaders used instrumental music to attract people back to Judaism. The community has borrowed and adapted to forge a new, distinctly Jewish music.

Gershom plays guitar and has recorded an album, *Sing for Joy: Abayudaya Jews of Uganda*. It is a combination of original and traditional songs. Noam Katz, a Reform rabbinic student and Jewish musician, spent three months volunteering with the Abayudaya. *Mirembe* is the album that came out of Noam's experience.

gershom's dream

Gershom said, "My dream is to make Africa Jewish..." Rabbi Sizomu opened yeshiva in Uganda to train Africa teachers and rabbis to serve growing Jewish communities throughout Africa.

The story of all the Jewish organizations and individuals who have helped the Abayudaya is a story of *Kol Yisrael aravim zeh ba-zeh*. Gershom's dedication of his life to his people is a statement of *ahavat Yisrael*.

Rabbi Jeffrey Summit, Hillel director and professor of music at Tufts, performed a labor of love in traveling to Uganda, taping the music and oral histories of this community and compiling it in a wonderful book and CD. Rabbi Summit quotes three communal leaders:

Israel Siriri told me: "We should continue to sing and teach our own melodies and traditions that have strengthened us over the years."

Uri Katula continued: "We need to sing our own traditional music. If not, there would be no need for you to come and see the Abayudaya. What would be the purpose? Would you be coming to learn? No. Because we would be doing what you do. And I doubt whether God likes that. Why did He place some Jews in Uganda and some in America? I think the purpose was to make it a colorful world."

Sizomu concluded, "We are one people, but like Joseph's coat, we are a coat of many colors."

1. What can we learn about *ahavat Yisrael* from the Abayudaya?
2. What does it mean "We...are like Joseph's coat; we are a coat of many colors"?

tzionut

The mountain where the Temple stood in Jerusalem was called *Tzion*. *Tzion* became another name for Israel. By 210 c.e. very few Jews lived in the land of Israel. Jews went into exile and were spread around the world. Immediately there was a desire to return.

The Passover seder ends with the words, "Next year in Jerusalem." In the siddur (prayer book) we find all kinds of calls for the return to Jerusalem, *Tzion* and Israel. These are all religious wishes. Even though there has been a new state of Israel since 1948, these wishes are still among the wishes we make in our prayers.

> Sound the shofar. Lift up the banner to bring our exiles together and assemble us from the four corners of the earth. Blessed are You, Eternal, who gathers the dispersed of our people Israel.
>
> Siddur, *Amidah*

In the late 1800s a political movement for the establishment of a new Jewish homeland in Palestine was started. Now that there is a State of Israel, *Tzionut*, Zionism, is about supporting and sustaining Israel. It is about making sure that there will always be an Israel.

PRAGUE, 1933. THE 18TH ZIONIST CONGRESS. © HASHOMER HATZAIR

Here are a number of Zionist quotations. Read each of them with a partner and explain what they mean.

Wherever I go, I go to Israel.
Rabbi Nachman of Bratzlov

The purpose of establishing Jewish settlements [in the land of Israel] is not to provide a living for a number of people, but to revive the spirit of our Holy Land; not to upbuild Palestine, but to bring into being the holiness of the Land of Israel.
Naftali Zvi Yehuda Berlin

Only in the Holy Land can the spirit of our people develop and become a light for the world.
Rabbi Abraham Isaac Kook (Rav Kook)

In Palestine we can and should find for ourselves a spiritual center of our nationality.
Ahad Ha'am

The State of Israel will prove itself not by material wealth, not by military might or technical achievement, but by its moral character and human values.
David Ben-Gurion

The Land of Israel was the birthplace of the Jewish people. Here their spiritual/religious and national identity was formed. Here they achieved independence and created a culture of national and universal significance...Jews strove throughout the centuries to go back to the land of their fathers and regain their statehood.
Israeli Declaration of Independence

1. What are some of the reasons that the State of Israel is important?

2. Why is *Tzionut* an important Jewish value?

42

tzionut hero: theodor herzl

Im tirzu ain zo agadah. "If you will it, it is no dream."

This is Theodor Herzl's most famous statement from his novel *Old-New Land.* In it he imagined the Jews living in Palestine as a free people with their own government. Within fifty years the State of Israel was born.

early life

Theodor Herzl (1860–1904) and his family spoke Hungarian and German, dressed like non-Jews and considered themselves Hungarians. As a teenager Herzl moved with his family to Vienna.

In his twenties Herzl became a writer and a journalist. In 1891 he covered the Dreyfus affair, a scandal involving a Jewish captain in the French army falsely accused of spying for Germany. Seeing great anti-Semitism, Herzl realized that no matter how deeply Jews felt French or German there would always be people who rejected them. He suggested that Jews needed a homeland of their own.

political zionism

Herzl wrote a booklet in 1896 called "The Jewish State: An Attempt at a Modern Solution to the Jewish Question". Herzl argued that the Jews should settle together in a country he called "the Promised Land" and create their own government. It would be "a state of Jews where no one has to be ashamed that he is a Jew."

In August 1897 Herzl organized the First Zionist Congress in Basel, Switzerland. One hundred ninety-seven Jews from fifteen countries attended. They represented different kinds of Jews from all over the world. What they had in common was the shared vision.

uganda

In 1902 Herzl published a novel about the future. It was called *Altneuland (Old New Land)* and it took place in Israel twenty years into the future. In it Herzl imagined turning Palestine into a Jewish State, the State of Israel. This fantasy gave Zionists hope that the hard work they were doing would lead to a positive future.

In 1903, the Government of Britain, offered Jews a chance to settle in Uganda, Africa. This caused a big fight in the Zionist movement. Some Jews felt that any Jewish State was better than no Jewish State. Others felt that *Eretz Yisrael*, the Land of Israel, was the only possible Jewish State. A third group argued, that Uganda was a good solution for now and Israel could happen later.

At the Sixth World Zionist Congress in Basel, Switzerland in 1903, the Uganda Question was debated and rejected. The majority opinion felt that Israel was the only place for a Jewish homeland. After this huge debate Herzl was exhausted.

israel

A year later, in 1904, Herzl died of pneumonia. He was buried in Vienna. Zionism went on. More and more Jews moved to Palestine (*Eretz Yisrael*) and settled there. In 1948, with a vote of the United Nations, Israel was declared a State. The long Zionist dream became a reality and Herzl was considered its father. In 1949 Herzl body was moved to Israel and buried on a high hill in Jerusalem. That hill was renamed Mount Herzl. In Israel, many things are named for Herzl, he was the one who started the effort that turned a long awaited Jewish dream into a reality.

tzionut text: excerpts from herzl's the jewish state

Theodor Herzl, the father of Zionism, outlined his vision for a Jewish state in *Der Judenstaat* (The Jewish State), published in February 1896. Here are some quotations from the pamphlet.

We Jews are a people—one people.

We have sincerely tried everywhere to merge with the national communities in which we live, seeking only to preserve the faith of our fathers. It is not permitted us... In our native lands where we have lived for centuries we are still treated as aliens, often by men whose ancestors had not yet arrived at the time when Jewish sighs had long been heard in the country.

Palestine is our unforgettable historic homeland...The Jews who will it shall achieve their State. We shall live at last as free men on our own soil, and in our own homes peacefully die. The world will be liberated by our freedom, enriched by our wealth, magnified by our greatness. And whatever we attempt there...will (be for) the good of all humankind.

1. What was Herzl's argument as to why Jews needed a state of Israel?
2. Does this argument hold up today?
3. Why is Herzl a *Tzionut* hero?

living tzionut

Some people say to be a Zionist one has to move to Israel. Others say that one has to support Israel. Still others say that one just has to love Israel.

What is your definition of a person who lives *Tzionut*?

Golda Meir (1898–1978) was born Golda Mabovitz in the Ukraine. When she was eight her family moved to the United States, fleeing pogroms. She grew up and was educated in Wisconsin. In 1921 she and her husband made *aliyah* to Israel, where Golda became one of the founders and great politicians of the emerging Jewish state. When they first moved to Israel, she and her husband Morris joined a kibbutz. On the kibbutz Golda Myerson (she had not yet changed her last name) was quickly elected to represent the kibbutz at the *Histadrut*, the General Federation of Labor. She was elected secretary of the Women's Labor Council in 1928. Through the following two decades she gained more and more prominence as a leader of the Zionist movement for the independence of Israel. In 1948 she was one of twenty-four signers of Israel's Declaration of Independence, and one of two women.

Golda said, "After I signed, I cried. When I studied American history as a schoolgirl and I read about those who signed the Declaration of Independence, I couldn't imagine these were real people doing something real. And there I was sitting down and signing a declaration of establishment." She first served as fundraiser in the U.S. for the fledgling Jewish state, having been issued Israel's first passport. Then she served as Israel's first ambassador to the Soviet Union.

From 1949–1974 she served as member of the Knesset, fulfilling a variety of roles, including foreign minister under Ben-Gurion. After the Six-Day War in 1968 she was called out of retirement to serve as prime minister. She was the first woman to be elected as head of Israel and only the third female prime minister ever in the world. Golda Meir resigned from the post of prime minister after the Yom Kippur War. She died in 1978.

"After I signed, I cried. When I studied American history as a schoolgirl and I read about those who signed the Declaration of Independence, I couldn't imagine these were real people doing something real. And there I was sitting down and signing a declaration of establishment."

tzionut activity: golda's speech

In January, 1948, Golda Meir flew to the United States to raise funds for the arms that were needed to defend the Jews in Palestine against the Arab attacks that were coming. All of the surrounding Arab nations were going to attack Israel.

Here is part of the speech that she made before the Council of Jewish Federations in Chicago on January 2, 1948. The Israeli Prime Minister, David Ben-Gurion, later described the result of her mission: "Someday when history will be written, it will be said that there was a Jewish woman who got the money which made the state possible."

> We always had faith that in the end we would win, that everything we were doing in the country led to the independence of the Jewish people and to a Jewish state. Long before we had dared pronounce that word, we knew what was in store for us...I want to say to you, friends, that the Jewish community in Palestine is going to fight to the very end. If we have arms to fight with, we will fight with those, and if not, we will fight with stones in our hands... During the last few years the Jewish people lost 6,000,000 Jews (in the Holocaust), and it would be an audacity [*hutzpah*] on our part to worry the Jewish people throughout the world because a few hundred thousand more Jews were in danger. That is not the issue. The issue is that if these 700,000 Jews in Palestine can remain alive, then the Jewish people is alive and Jewish independence is assured. If these 700,000 people are killed off, then for many centuries, we are through with this dream of a Jewish people and a Jewish homeland...

1. What was Golda Meir's mission in 1948?
2. What is her reason that the new State of Israel must survive?

ometz lev

Ometz means strength. *Lev* means heart. Strength of heart is usually understood as courage. This could be the bravery that David showed when he faced Goliath. But there are other kinds of *ometz lev*.

The *haftarah* for Ḥanukkah comes from Zechariah. Verse 4:6 says, "'NOT BY MIGHT, NOT BY POWER, BUT BY MY SPIRIT' SAID THE ETERNAL OF HOSTS." It teaches us that one Jewish understanding of courage is faith in God. Think of the famous text from Psalm 23:4 "THOUGH I WALK THROUGH A VALLEY OF DEEPEST DARKNESS, I FEAR NO HARM, FOR YOU ARE WITH ME. YOUR ROD AND YOUR STAFF—THEY COMFORT ME." Here we have the same idea again—that connection to God can be a source of strength.

Many Jews have shown *ometz lev* in battle or in moments that saved Jewish lives. But there is a different kind of *ometz lev*—the courage to take control of one's self and become the best possible person one can be. In *Pirkei Avot* (4:1) we learn, "Who is strong? One who conquers one's own worst tendencies." One can show *ometz lev* in dramatic moments, and one can live *ometz lev* everyday.

47

ometz lev: text

David said to Do'eg (someone who betrayed him): "WHY, STRONG ONE, DO YOU BRAG ABOUT EVIL?" (Psalms 52:3)

Are you strong if you see someone on the edge of a pit and push that person in? Or are you strong if you find someone on the roof of a building and push this person off? Is this strength? When can someone truly be called "mighty"?

When someone is about to fall into a pit, a strong person takes that person's hand and prevents that person from falling in. When someone has fallen into a pit, a strong person lifts that person out. (*Midrash Tehillim 56:2*)

1. What does this text teach us about *ometz lev*?

2. Who do you know of who lives up to this standard?

early life

Regina Jonas was born on August 3, 1902 in Berlin, Germany. The family was Orthodox and came from Eastern Europe. Her father, Wolf, died in 1913. He left his widow, Sarah, and two children penniless.

The family moved to a new apartment. The small Orthodox synagogue next door changed Regina's life. She was attracted to the synagogue and the rabbi, Dr. Max Weil, who was one of the first in Germany to conduct bat mitzvah ceremonies. The rabbi took Regina under his wing. He was the one who paved the way for her studies, first in a Jewish school and afterward in the *Hochschule* (high school). In 1930 she was certified as a teacher and began to support herself and her mother as a Judaic studies teacher.

rabbi jonas

Jonas never married and lived with her mother her whole life. She lived as an Orthodox Jew, yet she studied at the *Hochschule für die Wissenschaft des Judentums*, the College for the Science of Judaism, which was considered liberal. She believed there was no contradiction between *halakhah* (Jewish religious law) and her desire to serve in the rabbinate. After completing her teaching certification she continued to study. She wrote a paper discussing the question "Can a woman be a rabbi?" Her answer was "Yes."

Her teachers praised her dissertation, but none of them agreed to ordain her. In 1935, at the request of the Union of Liberal Rabbis in Germany, Regina Jonas was ordained by

Max Dienemann, a liberal rabbi. She was the first female rabbi. After her ordination Rabbi Leo Baeck sent her a letter of congratulation, and in 1942 he added his signature to her ordination certificate. She was unable to find a congregation to hire her as a rabbi. She served only in old age homes and hospitals.

After *Kristallnacht* ("The Night of Broken Glass") in November 1938, Regina Jonas preached in various synagogues in Berlin, often replacing rabbis who were in concentration camps or had escaped Germany.

waiting for the trains

In 1942 Rabbi Jonas was sent to Theresienstadt, a Nazi concentration camp. Even though many in Berlin had failed to accept her as a rabbi, there she worked as a rabbi. She worked as a counselor and a teacher. Dr. Viktor Frankl, a famous psychiatrist, had a team that worked in Theresienstadt to protect the mental health of those in the camp. Both Rabbi Regina Jonas and Rabbi Leo Baeck were on his team. She showed *Ometz Lev* and did important work. In 1944 she and her mother were sent to Auschwitz. They died there.

forgotten and then celebrated

Somehow, Rabbi Jonas was forgotten until 1991. No one had told her story or included her in the telling of the story of the Holocaust. People thought that Rabbi Sally Priesand, who was ordained in 1972 by the Hebrew Union College, was the first woman rabbi. In 1991 East and West Germany united and Jews got access to the files of the *Hochschule*. There one of the researchers found a file with papers by and a photograph of Rabbi Regina Jonas. Suddenly her story was recovered.

ometz lev text: eyewitness testimony

A Holocaust survivor said this about Rabbi Jonas:

> In Berlin there lived at this time in the 1930s the first woman rabbi, Fraulein Rabbiner Regina Jonas. She watched carefully that one said "Fraulein Rabbiner," because a "frau rabbiner" was the wife of a rabbi. She came into the hospital and old age home very often, and there she wanted to function as a rabbi. Generally, this worked in the old age home and in the hospital. When she came into the synagogue wearing a purple robe—not black—she sat herself downstairs next to the men on the rabbi's seat. She wanted to give her lecture or sermon during the prayers, but always when this doctor was there and prayed with the people, he said to her, "You can do what you want, but for the prayers you go upstairs to the women, and afterwards you can come downstairs."

1. How do you think it felt for Rabbi Jonas not to get respect as a rabbi?
2. How did she demonstrate *ometz lev?*

ometz lev hero: rabbi leo baeck

Leo Baeck (1873–1956) was an important liberal Jewish theologian, who thought and wrote about God. He also showed *ometz lev* as a hero of the Holocaust.

student, teacher, rabbi

Leo Baeck was born in the German town of Lissa. Samuel Baeck, his father, was a local rabbi. Leo was brought up keeping kosher and studying Talmud. His father had a friendship with the local Christian minister. This friendship taught Leo Baeck to appreciate interfaith friendship and dialogue.

Leo Baeck enrolled in the The Jewish Theological Seminary of Breslau, a Conservative rabbinical academy. In 1894 Baeck left JTS for Berlin's Reform-oriented Hochschule für die Wissenschaft des Judentums—the College for the Science of Judaism. There he received his rabbinic diploma in 1897.

During World War I Leo Baeck was a military chaplain and serviced on both the eastern and western fronts. In addition to ministering to the troops, he saw to the spiritual needs of local Russian Jews.

baeck's theology: the essence of judaism

Leo Baeck thought of Judaism as the universal religion of reason. He was less concerned with the idea of God than with his congregants' real-life spiritual experiences. His best-known work was *The Essence of Judaism*.

baeck and the nazis

Rabbi Baeck was sought out for positions of communal leadership. He was a member of the Central Association of German Citizens of Jewish Faith, an organization committed to fighting German anti-Semitism. After Hitler's rise to power Baeck refused all offers of escape, declaring that he would stay as long as there was a minyan of

Jews in Germany. In 1933 he was elected founding president of the Representative Council of German Jews. He fought against the Nazis, working to provide social services to the survivors of the Jewish community and often negotiating directly with the Nazis.

theresienstadt

In 1943 Leo Baeck was deported to Theresienstadt concentration camp in Czechoslovakia. There he was put to physical labor pushing a garbage cart. Baeck was elected honorary president of the camp's Jewish Council of Elders. He worked hard to preserve the humanity of those around him and ministered to Jewish and Christian inmates alike. Baeck took every opportunity to continue his work as a rabbi and scholar. He would discuss philosophy with fellow prisoners while he pushed his garbage cart around camp. In the evenings hundreds of people would crowd into a small barracks to hear Baeck lecturing from memory on famous philosophers like Herodotus, Plato and Kant.

After the liberation of Theresienstadt in May 1945, Baeck prevented the camp's inmates from killing the guards. He then stayed on to counsel the sick and the dying.

after the war

Rabbi Baeck went to London where he eventually became the chairman of the World Union for Progressive Judaism. He also lectured from time to time at the Hebrew Union College in Cincinnati. Rabbi Baeck did not give up his belief in God or Judaism during the Holocaust. He explained that the awful things that happened there were not the failure of God, but the failure of human beings. Both during and after the Holocaust he lived a life of *ometz lev*. A rabbinic school in London, a synagogue in Los Angeles, and an educational complex in Haifa are some places named after him.

ometz lev: an ethical dilemma

Leo Baeck was one of the leaders of the German Jewish community until he was sent to the Theresienstadt in 1943. People were moved from there to Auschwitz, a death camp. Somewhere during that time he received word that the Nazis were killing million of Jews in death camps. Theresienstadt was a concentration camp. Dr. Baeck decided to keep the knowledge of these death camps a secret. He explained:

"Living in the expectation of death by gassing would be all the harder. And this death was not certain for all...So 1 came to the grave decision to tell no one."

1. Why do you think Rabbi Baeck did not tell others about the death camps?
2. Do you think that not telling about the death camps was the right thing?
3. In what ways did Rabbi Leo Baeck demonstrate *ometz lev* in his life?

showing ometz lev

Both of our *ometz lev* heroes were heroes of the Holocaust, but people show courage in all kinds of ways.

4. Who do you think shows *ometz lev*?
5. What did he or she do?
6. When is a time when you showed *ometz lev*?

THERESIENSTADT CONCENTRATION CAMP IN THE CZECH REPUBLIC

tzedek tzedek tirdof

The Torah says, "*Tzedek tzedek tirdof,* JUSTICE, JUSTICE SHALL YOU PURSUE, SO THAT YOU MAY LIVE AND INHERIT THE LAND THAT THE ETERNAL YOUR GOD GIVES YOU" (Deuteronomy 16:20). *Tzedek,* "justice," is a core Jewish value. For example, while Jews have 613 mitzvot to follow, non-Jews have only seven. One of the seven things that the Jewish tradition teaches that non-Jews need to do in order to be ethical is have just courts (*Mishneh Torah, Book of Judges, Laws of Kings 9:1*).

The Jewish commitment to justice starts with Abraham. First God reflects on telling Abraham what is about to happen to Sodom and Gomorrah. God says: "FOR I HAVE KNOWN HIM SO THAT HE MAY COMMAND HIS CHILDREN...TO DO RIGHTEOUSNESS AND JUSTICE..." (Genesis 18:19). Then Abraham told God, "SHALL NOT THE JUDGE OF ALL THE EARTH DO JUSTLY?" (Genesis 18:25). Justice is at the heart of the Jewish relationship with God.

Justice, of course, has to do with courts and laws. That is one kind of justice. Another kind of justice has to do with the way we treat other people. That is why the word *tzedakah* comes from the root *tzedek,* justice. Micah the prophet taught us: "It has been told you, human, what is good, and what the Eternal does demand of you: only to seek justice, and to love mercy, and to walk humbly with your God."

tzedek tzedek tirdof text: nahmanides

The Torah says:

AND YOU SHALL DO WHAT IS RIGHT AND GOOD IN THE SIGHT OF THE ETERNAL, THAT IT MAY GO WELL WITH YOU, AND THAT YOU MAY GO IN AND TAKE POSSESSION OF THE GOOD LAND THAT THE ETERNAL SWORE TO GIVE TO YOUR FATHERS.

Deuteronomy 6:18

Nahmanides explains it:

In Deuteronomy 6:17 God says, "YOU SHALL DILIGENTLY KEEP THE MITZVOT OF THE ETERNAL YOUR GOD, AND GOD'S RULES, AND GOD'S ORDINANCES, THAT HAVE BEEN COMMANDED YOU." The next verse, "AND YOU SHALL DO WHAT IS RIGHT AND GOOD IN THE SIGHT OF THE ETERNAL," goes beyond specific rules. It speaks of compromise and actions that are beyond the obligations of the law. God first tells you to obey the law; then God reminds you to do what is "RIGHT AND GOOD" when it is beyond the law.

This is a great matter. It is impossible to mention in the Torah all of a person's actions toward his neighbors and friends...So after God has mentioned many of them...God continues to say that even if it is not specifically mentioned, one should still do "WHAT IS RIGHT AND GOOD" through compromises and other actions that are specifically mentioned in the Torah.

Commentary on the Torah, Deuteronomy 6:18

1. What does Nahmanides say is the difference between Deuteronomy 6:17 and Deuteronomy 6:18?

2. What does he mean when he says God also wants us to do "'RIGHT AND GOOD' when it is beyond the law"?

3. Give an example of something that is "RIGHT AND GOOD" and beyond the law.

tzedek tzedek tirdof hero: justice louis brandeis

Louis D. Brandeis was the first Jew to serve on the Supreme Court. He was an early supporter of Israel and helped immigrants in New York City's poor neighborhoods. His influence was so great that two schools—Brandeis University in Waltham, MA, and the Brandeis School of Law at the University of Louisville—bear his name.

beginnings

Louis D. Brandeis was born in 1856 in Louisville, Kentucky, to parents who had emigrated from Prague. His parents believed in hard work and taught him how important it was to learn. His family was not very religious. Louis did not have a bar mitzvah, and he did not set foot in a synagogue until much later in his life.

Louis' hero was his uncle, Lewis Dembitz, who was a lawyer active in politics. He encouraged his nephew to attend the Annen Realschule, a prestigious high school in Germany. Louis loved school and was able to get into Harvard Law School, where he was a spectacular student.

the people's attorney

One of his first big cases was in 1907. Lawmakers in Oregon wanted to make conditions better for workers, so they passed some new laws. One of those laws made it illegal for women to work too many hours in a week. Poor women often worked because their families needed the money. Because they were desperate for jobs, they ended up having to work very long hours. A man who owned a laundry business in Portland didn't like the law. He thought that he should be able to hire his employees for as many hours as they were willing to work. He got in trouble for violating Oregon's law. The state of Oregon hired Louis D. Brandeis. The case came before the U.S. Supreme Court as *Muller* v. *Oregon*. The case made Brandeis famous. Many groups wanted to hire him to represent workers in cases against their bosses. In 1910 a group of garment workers in New York tried to get better treatment from factory owners. They held a strike until their demands were met. Louis Brandeis was brought in to mediate the strike. He became known as the "People's Attorney," because he believed in representing everyone.

brandeis discovers judaism

Even though he was Jewish, Brandeis did not know very many Jews. He thought of Judaism as just a religion. He didn't even consider himself very Jewish. The experience with the garment workers exposed him to the large Jewish population that had settled in New York. Brandeis began to understand about Jews being part of a nation. Around the same time Brandeis was introduced to Jacob de Haas and Aaron Aaronsohn. Aaronsohn was a botanist who lived in Palestine, and de Haas was a prominent English Jew. The two men were Zionists. Along with their friend Rabbi Stephen Wise, they turned Brandeis into a Zionist.

brandeis and the supreme court

In 1916 a spot opened up on the Supreme Court. President Wilson picked the best lawyer he knew: Louis Brandeis. Wilson's choice surprised a lot of people. Supreme Court justices are usually judges first. Most Supreme Court justices were old men who didn't believe in making big changes.

Brandeis had many enemies and they tried to influence the Senate to not approve Brandeis. One senator said, "[Brandeis] is a Hebrew...some of his ideas might not be the same as those of a man possessing an Anglo-Saxon mind." The anti-Semitic attacks hurt Brandeis. He was proud of his intelligence, and he was just as proud of being Jewish. Being told his ideas weren't good enough because he was Jewish was very hurtful.

Brandeis was sworn in as a Supreme Court justice on June 4, 1916 and served until Feb. 13, 1939. He died on October 5, 1941.

tzedek tzedek tirdof activity:
the ethics of judge louis d. brandeis

Louis D. Brandeis "refused to serve (as a lawyer) in a cause that he considered bad." When Brandeis believed that his clients were wrong, "either he would persuade his clients to make amends...or he would withdraw from the case."

Diana Klebanow and Franklin L Jonas in a People's Lawyers: Crusaders for Justice in American History.

One time he was unsure of whether his client was right, he wrote the client, "The position that I should take if I remained in the case would be to give everybody a square deal."

Thomas A. Mason, Brandeis: A Free Man's Life

American Law is based on the idea that each side needs a lawyer to represent their case. The two lawyers do their best and in the conflict the truth comes out. A Jewish court (Bet Din) doesn't use lawyers. It has three judges and they ask the questions and argue to a decision. Justice Brandeis was an American lawyer.

1. Do you think his decision not to work on cases in which he believed his client was wrong was a good decision?

2. Should every position have a lawyer?

3. Should a lawyer represent every position?

tzedek tzedek tirdof hero: rabbi abraham joshua heschel

Not all justice happens in the courtroom or the Congress. Some of it happens on the street. Abraham Joshua Heschel lived *tzedek tzedek tirdof.*

the early years

Abraham Joshua Heschel was born in 1907 in Warsaw, Poland. In his teens Heschel received a traditional yeshiva education and obtained rabbinic ordination. He then studied at the University of Berlin, where he obtained his doctorate and earned a second liberal rabbinic ordination at the *Hochschule für die Wissenschaft des Judentums.*

In 1939 World War II began. Many countries—among them Britain, France, the United States and Russia—were drawn into the war against the Nazis. Deported to Poland by the Nazis in 1938, Heschel taught for eight months at the Warsaw Institute of Jewish Studies. He then emigrated to England, where he established the Institute for Jewish Learning in London.

In 1940 he came to the Hebrew Union College in Cincinnati (the main seminary for Reform Judaism), where he became associate professor of philosophy and rabbinics until the end of the war. In 1946 he came to the Conservative movement's Jewish Theological Seminary of America.

Heschel was a noted author of texts on Jewish life, including *The Sabbath: Its Meaning for Modern Man, Man is Not Alone: A Philosophy of Religion* and *God in Search of Man: A Philosophy of Judaism.*

social justice

Heschel had a major disagreement with much of the Jewish Theological Seminary faculty due to his views on the Hebrew prophets and social justice. He saw the teachings of the Hebrew prophets as a loud call for social action in the United States. Most of the faculty saw their job as academics and educators, and they left the world of social activism to pulpit rabbis and lay people.

Heschel was active in the civil rights movement and marched with Martin Luther King, Jr. in the protest march at Selma, Alabama. He described the march in these words: "For many of us the march from Selma to Montgomery was both protest and prayer. Our legs uttered songs. I felt my legs were praying."

CIVIL RIGHTS LEADERS RALPH ABERNATHY, MARTIN LUTHER KING, JR., FORMER UNITED NATIONS AMBASSADOR RALPH BUNCHE AND RABBI ABRAHAM JOSHUA HESCHEL (L-R) AT THE START OF A MARCH FROM SELMA TO MONTGOMERY, ALABAMA.

Heschel spoke out for peace. He helped organize and served as co-chair of Clergy and Laity Concerned about Vietnam, a group that represented the religious opposition to the war in Vietnam.

Heschel died on December 23, 1972. Four day schools and various organizations are named for him. Abraham Joshua Heschel taught the prophets and lived up to their ethical demands. He lived *tzedek tzedek tirdof.*

Here are four quotations by Rabbi Abraham Joshua Heschel.

[a] A religious man is a person who holds God and man in one thought at one time, at all times, who suffers harm done to others, whose greatest passion is compassion, whose greatest strength is love and defiance of despair.

[b] When I was young, I admired clever people. Now that I am old, I admire kind people.

[c] There are inalienable obligations as well as inalienable rights.

[d] A person cannot be religious and indifferent to other human beings' plight and suffering. In fact, the tragedy of humankind is that so much of our history is a history of indifference, dominated by a famous statement, Am I my brother's keeper?

11/20/1963— ABRAHAM JOSHUA HESCHEL (R) ASSISTS GEORGE MAISLEN (L), PRESIDENT OF THE UNITED SYNAGOGUE OF AMERICA, IN PRESENTING THE SOLOMON SCHECHTER AWARD TO REVEREND DR. MARTIN LUTHER KING JR. (C), "FOR TRANSLATING THE PROPHETIC VISION OF ABRAHAM LINCOLN INTO A LIVING REALITY."

1. Which text do you like best?
2. What lesson does it teach you?
3. What does Heschel teach us about *tzedek tzedek tirdof*?

being like heschel

Heschel lived a life of Torah and pursuing justice. He stood up for things that in his day needed standing up for. What are three just things that people need to pursue today?

4. _____

5. _____

6. _____

t'shuvah

If you want to become a good person, two of the most important skills you need are (1) being able to say to yourself and to another person, "I am wrong," and (2) being able to say to yourself, "I am willing to change so that this will never happen again." *T'shuvah* is the way that Jews work on both of these.

T'shuvah is a solution. When you have done something wrong, when you have hurt someone else or hurt yourself—and you are unhappy with the way you have acted—*t'shuvah* is the solution.

תְּשׁוּבָה *T'shuvah* comes from the Hebrew word שׁוּב, *shuv*, which means "to turn". *T'shuvah* is usually translated as "repent". The "re" part has to do with starting over again. But *t'shuvah* is better understood as returning to friendship with the person you hurt and returning to closeness with God, Who was also hurt by your actions. However, the best understanding of *t'shuvah* is getting back on the path toward becoming the best you that you can become.

t'shuvah text: saadia gaon

Saadia Gaon taught that t'shuvah has four steps.

A. **Confession:** admitting that you have done wrong and stating that you will never repeat the action.

B. **Remorse:** feeling bad about the hurt you have caused.

C. **Seeking forgiveness:** asking the person you have wronged to forgive you. Also, asking God to forgive you.

D. **Accepting Responsibility:** finding your own way to never repeat this action.

(*The Book of Beliefs and Opinions* 5:5)

1. According to Saadia, what is the difference between saying "I'm sorry" and doing *t'shuvah*?

2. How does this definition help us see *t'shuvah* as "return"?

t'shuvah hero: rabbi mark borovitz

Mark Borovitz is an alcoholic. Mark teaches that even if you are a recovered alcoholic, you are always an alcoholic. Today Rabbi Borovitz is the rabbi of Beit T'Shuvah, a halfway house for Jews in recovery. Mark not only did *t'shuvah*, he now devotes his life to helping others do *t'shuvah*. Here is Mark's story in his own words from *T'shuvah: "Carry the Message of Jewish Recovery,"* September 1992.

mock butts

One day when I was three I "did a geographic". My parents were gone, my brothers were supposed to be watching me. I went for a walk around the block...The police from a different suburb found me and took me to their station. They took me in because I couldn't say my name or give my address. The only thing I could tell the police was that I was Mock Butts. That was as close to my name as I could come.

When my father did find me, his response to "Mock Butts" was to laugh and say, "That's my boy, a real Mock Butts." I remember his laugh showing love and caring. I spent the next thirty-four years trying to find more of that kind of love and affection.

drunk bar mitzvah

The next thing I remember was getting drunk at my brother's bar mitzvah. Everyone thought I was cute. I got a lot of attention, and no one really got mad. I wasn't afraid of anything. From then on I was on a downward spiral, just like a real alcoholic.

My next thirty years consisted of chasing the people who didn't want me and screwing the people who did. I stole money from my mother's purse (and we couldn't afford that) to buy things for people, or to just pay them to be my friends.

My father died when I was fourteen, and my world ended...I was supposed to be the "man of the house." I didn't want the job. But I provided them with a lot of money, and I took away a lot with all the trouble I caused.

going "geographic" again

In 1976 I got in major trouble again. I had dropped out of college and worked at lots of jobs. Some

were legal; most weren't. I was facing a problem for which some people wanted to hurt me. I was lucky that there was someone around who still liked me. My brother, who was in California, suggested that a road trip could lead to a new start. I moved to L.A., but nothing changed. I hit bottom. I got arrested for DUIs (driving under the influence) and NSF (non-sufficient funds) checks and even for grand thefts. I married a woman I did not love and had a daughter. I didn't even know what love was. I was in and out of jails and prisons for the next seven years.

In 1986 I was on my way to Las Vegas to bet on football and win enough money to pay off my bad checks and get myself out of jail. A cop who had arrested me before knew I had outstanding warrants and busted me again. I went to jail. God has a sense of humor. All my teams won. I would have won more than $50,000 and gotten out of trouble. Instead I was in jail.

speaking to god

In jail I was finally able to hear God speak. Suddenly I knew that I was supposed to fix my life. I asked to see the prison rabbi...It took him a while to get to me...When he finally showed up and I told him that I felt rejected, Rabbi Mel Silverman said to me, "How could I cut you loose? You are one of my own." Everything started to change at that moment. That was the beginning of my return.

Since then I got clean and I got out of jail. I found a wife and continued to study. I am a rabbi and spend most of my time helping other addicts to recover and helping kids not to start. Not bad for "Mock Butts."

t'shuvah text: mark's favorite story

This story is one of Mark's favorite teachings.

Once the great Ḥasidic rabbi Zusya came to his followers upset.

They asked, "Reb Zusya, what's the matter? You look frightened!"

He answered, "I had a vision. In it I learned the question that the angels will one day ask me about my life."

The followers were puzzled. "Zusya, you are a good Jew. You are scholarly and humble. What question about your life could be so terrifying that you would be frightened to answer it?"

Zusya said, "I have learned that the angels will not ask me, 'Why weren't you a Moses, leading your people out of slavery?'"

His followers persisted. "So what will they ask you?"

"And I have learned," Zusya sighed, "that the angels will not ask me, 'Why weren't you a Joshua, leading your people into the Promised Land?'"

"But what will they ask you?"

"They will say to me, 'Why weren't you the best possible Zusya?'"

1. What lesson does this story teach?
2. How is it a story about *t'shuvah*?
3. How can you be the best you?

your t'shuvah

You may not be an alcoholic or a drug addict, but everyone has a list of things they need to do *t'shuvah* about. What are three things on your list?

4. _____

5. _____

6. _____

> "More change for the better took place in his twenty-seven-year papacy than in the nearly two thousand years before."

Pope John Paul II was a Catholic, but his biography includes one story that is important to Jews.

karol jozef wojtyla

Pope John Paul II was born Karol Jozef Wojtyla in the Polish town of Wadowice, a small city fifty kilometers from Krakow. He reigned as Pope from October 16, 1978 until his death almost twenty-seven years later.

his catholic story

He was baptized on June 20, 1920 in the parish church of Wadowice, made his First Holy Communion at age nine and was confirmed at eighteen. Upon graduation from Marcin Wadowita high school he enrolled at Krakow's university in 1938. The Nazi occupation forces closed the university in 1939, and young Karol had to work in a quarry and then in the Solvay chemical factory to earn his living.

In 1942, deciding to be a priest, he began courses in the underground seminary of Krakow. He was ordained to the priesthood on November 1, 1946. After years of service to the Catholic Church, he was elected Pope by the Cardinals at the Conclave of October 16, 1978. He took the name John Paul II.

his jewish story

From the beginning, relationships between the Catholic Church and the Jewish people have not been good. The Church had often been guilty of anti-Semitism and was seen as silent during the Holocaust. Pope John Paul II set out to heal this relationship. In 1979 he became the first Pope to visit the Auschwitz concentration camp in Poland. In 1998 he issued *We Remember: A Reflection on the Shoah* (Holocaust). He also became the first pope known to have made an official visit to a synagogue.

In 1994, in honor of the establishment of diplomatic relations between the Vatican and the State of Israel, Pope John Paul II hosted the Papal Concert to Commemorate the Holocaust. In March 2000 John Paul II visited Yad Vashem, the Israeli national Holocaust memorial, and later made history by touching the Western Wall (*ha-Kotel*) and placing a letter in it. The letter was a prayer for forgiveness for actions against Jews in the past.

Immediately after the pope's death the Anti-Defamation League issued a statement that Pope John Paul II had revolutionized Catholic–Jewish relations, saying that "more change for the better took place in his twenty-seven-year papacy than in the nearly two thousand years before."

Here is the speech of Pope John Paul II during his visit to Yad Vashem, Thursday, March 23, 2000:

...As Bishop of Rome and Successor of the Apostle Peter, I assure the Jewish people that the Catholic Church, motivated by the Gospel law of truth and love...is deeply saddened by the hatred, acts of persecution and displays of anti-Semitism directed against the Jews by Christians at any time and in any place. The Church rejects racism in any form as a denial of the image of the Creator present in every human being (cf. *Gen* 1:26).

In this place of solemn remembrance, I fervently pray that our sorrow for the tragedy that the Jewish people suffered in the twentieth century will lead to a new relationship between Christians and Jews. Let us build a new future in which there will be no more anti-Jewish feeling among Christians or anti-Christian feeling among Jews, but rather the mutual respect required of those who adore the one Creator and Eternal, and look to Abraham as our common father in faith.

1. What is special about this speech?
2. How is it a model for *t'shuvah*?

anavah

value: anavah

God has told you, human, what is good and what God requires of you: To seek justice, love goodness, and walk humbly with your God. (Micah 6:8)

Anavah means humility. The Jewish tradition is big on humility. Humility is not feeling bad about yourself. It is not disliking yourself. Rather, it is not making yourself too important. The 13th- 14th-century teacher Bahya ben Asher said, "Humility is halfway between too much pride and too little pride. It does not mean that we should disgrace ourselves or allow others to walk over us. Because we are created in God's image, we are precious. We need to care for our honor and the high status that a rational soul gave us among God's creatures." (*Kad ha-Kemah*)

Rabbi Simhah Bunam of Przysucha once taught that we should keep two pieces of paper in our pockets, one saying "For my sake the world was created" and the other "I am nothing but dust and ashes." Whenever we are overcome by feelings of pride, he said, we should read the paper with the words "I am nothing but dust and ashes." And when we feel shame and as if our sense of self has been destroyed, we should reach into the other pocket and read "For my sake the world was created." Here we learn to balance pride with humility.

Here are three Rabbinic texts about anavah. Restate each one in your own words.

[1]

Be very humble, because the end of a person is worms.

Pirkei Avot 4:4

[2]

Why were human beings created on a Friday? So that if they become too much for themselves, one can say to them, "The mosquito was created before you."

Sanhedrin 38a

[3]

Let a person always be humble in Torah and good works, humble with parents, teachers, spouse and children, with a household and relatives near and far, even with strangers in the street, so that person will be loved on high and be desired on earth.

Tanna de Be Eliyahu, p. 197

anavah hero: albert einstein

Two interesting facts about Einstein: first, he never wore socks. He said, "When I was young, I found out that the big toe always ends up making a hole in the sock. So I stopped wearing socks." Second, he could take off his vest without removing his jacket. It was his favorite trick.

early life

Albert Einstein was born at Württemberg, Germany, on March 14, 1879. In 1933 he gave up his citizenship for political reasons and moved to America. In 1933 Hilter came to power and the Nazi era began. Einstein became a professor of theoretical physics at Princeton. He became a United States citizen in 1940.

zionism

Einstein was a Zionist. After World War II he was offered the presidency of the State of Israel, but he said no. Einstein wrote to Abba Eban and said, "All my life I have dealt with objective matters; hence I lack both the experience to deal properly with people and to carry out official functions." It was a humble response.

physics

Albert Einstein spent his life trying to figure out how the universe works. He used to say, "God doesn't play dice with the universe." In other words, there are rules by which the world was created. He believed it was our job to figure them out.

the atom bomb

Albert Einstein did not directly participate in the creation of the atomic bomb, but he was important to its development. His greatest role in the invention of the atomic bomb was the signing of a letter to President Franklin Roosevelt urging that the bomb be built because the Nazis were working on their own bomb.

After the war Einstein wrote, "I made one great mistake in my life...when I signed the letter to President Roosevelt recommending that atom bombs be made; but there was some justification—the danger that the Germans would make them." Einstein was able to admit that he was wrong. This was part of being a scientist. He said, "Anyone who has never made a mistake has never tried anything new."

humility

We can see Einstein's humility in his words. As a very famous person he said things like "The only way to escape the corruptible effects of praise is to go on working." Also, "I have no special talents. I am only passionately curious." Despite all of his fame, despite all of his importance, Einstein saw himself as a simple man, a scientist. He lived a life of *anavah*.

albert einstein text

Paolo Mazzilli said the following about Albert Einstein:

We all need a bit of Einstein's genius, to perceive better the secrets of the Universe.

We all need a bit of Einstein's brotherhood spirit, to despise the war all over the world.

We all need a bit of Einstein's humility, to be able to perceive the existence of God.

1. According to Paolo Mazzilli, what three things can we learn from Albert Einstein?

2. In what three ways do we need to be like Einstein?

anavah hero: moses

the problem

He was "a prince of Egypt" and the guy chosen by God to lead the Jewish people. He led 600,000 people, got the Ten Commandments and was called to the burning bush. Still he wrote in the Torah about himself, "THE MAN, MOSES, WAS VERY HUMBLE, MORE THAN ANY OTHER PERSON ON THE FACE OF THE EARTH." (Numbers 12:3)

the calling

Moses was raised in Pharaoh's palace. He sew a Jew being beaten by an Egyptian. When he stepped in and stopped the beating, some Jews threatened to turn him in. He ran. Moses came to Midian, where he was considered to be an Egyptian. He got a job as a shepherd. A shepherd is very different from a prince.

One day God showed up, did some special effects with a bush and asked Moses to lead the Jewish people out of Egypt. Moses' response was not "They don't want me." It wasn't "I'm not really a Jew." Instead he said, "WHO AM I, THAT I SHOULD GO TO PHARAOH, AND THAT I SHOULD BRING THE FAMILIES-OF-ISRAEL OUT OF EGYPT?" (Exodus 3:11). In other words, "I am a nobody."

delegating

Moses led the Jewish people out of Egypt. He held up his staff, and the Reed Sea divided. They were now camped in freedom. His father-in-law Jethro showed up and suggested to Moses that his workload could be reduced through the appointment of "LEADERS OVER THOUSANDS, HUNDREDS, FIFTIES, AND TENS'" (Exod. 18:21). Instead of rejecting the suggestion, instead of saying, "I am in charge," instead of saying no, Moses listened to the idea.

Later God gave Moses more help by sharing the Holy Spirit with seventy of Israel's elders (Num. 11:24-25). When two of the elders "PROPHESIED IN THE CAMP" Joshua told Moses to stop them, but it didn't bother Moses. He had no need to be the only prophet. Instead he said, "ARE YOU JEALOUS FOR ME? WOULD THAT ALL THE ETERNAL'S PEOPLE WERE PROPHETS, THAT THE ETERNAL WOULD PUT GOD'S SPIRIT ON THEM!" (Numbers 11:29). He did not view the prophesying of Eldad and Medad as a threat.

conflict

Aaron and Miriam were Moses' brother and sister. There is a time when they both yelled at Moses and attacked his leadership (Numbers 12:1-2). They said, "HAS THE ETERNAL SPOKEN ONLY THROUGH MOSES? HAS GOD NOT SPOKEN THROUGH US ALSO?" Moses did not respond to the attack. Instead, the Torah says, "THE MAN, MOSES, WAS VERY HUMBLE, MORE THAN ANY OTHER PERSON ON THE FACE OF THE EARTH." Moses said nothing, God stepped in, then Moses asked God that Miriam's punishment be stopped. Pretty humble!

Twice, when God was angry at the Families-of-Israel, God threatened to destroy the Jewish people and start over building a nation through Moses (Exodus 32:9-10; Numbers 14:11-12). Each time Moses talked God down. He cared more for Israel than for his own future.

moses' humility

Anavah is not weakness. The Talmud says, "Any place where one finds the strength, there one finds humility" (Megillah 31a). The secret to Moses is that he was both strong and humble. When you are confident you don't need to overreact. That is the *anavah* we can learn from Moses.

anavah text

Rav Abraham Isaac Kook was the first Chief Rabbi of Israel. He wrote the following about *anavah*. It helps us to understand more about Moses.

People can find in themselves high, great and important qualities. They can also find low and mean qualities.

People see themselves as lowly because of their negative qualities and of high value because of their good qualities.

But they must not boast of their good qualities. Just the opposite, even their good qualities should fill them with endless humility, for it is the good qualities that challenge them to develop their other qualities that are in an undeveloped state.

1. What can good qualities do?
2. What can bad qualities do?
3. Why should a person be humble about the good qualities?
4. How is this the story of Moses?

kiddush ha-shem

kiddush

You probably know the *Kiddush* as the blessing we say over wine. The actual Hebrew word *kiddush* means "holy". *Kiddush* is when we use a glass of wine (or grape juice) to recognize the holiness of Shabbat (or other holidays). The wine is something concrete that helps us appreciate Shabbat, which is something we can't touch or sense. *Kiddush* really means "set apart," just as the Shabbat is set apart from the weekdays.

ha-shem

Ha-Shem means "the Name" and refers to God's name. Judaism makes a big deal out of God's name. God's actual name is made up of four letters, *hey, vav, hey, yud*. No one knows how to pronounce it. We use the word *Adonai* (Our Master) instead, leaving "the Name" unpronounced. Some Jews say *ha-Shem* instead of *Adonai* when they are talking and not praying.

two kinds of kiddush ha-shem

Kiddush ha-Shem means "Making the Name Holy." It has two different meanings. It is *kiddush ha-Shem* when someone gives up his or her life in a way that gives honor to the Jewish people and God. One who sacrifices his or her life for others or for a cause is called a martyr. Judaism is not big or martyrdom but believes that there are times when it is necessary. The other meaning of *kiddush ha-Shem* is not dying, but living in a way that gives honor to God and the Jewish people. Both ways give dignity to the Jewish people and reflect well on God, showing that God makes a difference.

71

The *Shema* (*V'Ahavta*) commands us to LOVE GOD WITH ALL OUR HEART, ALL OUR SOUL, AND ALL OUR MIGHT. Rabbi Akiva teaches: "'WITH ALL THY SOUL' means 'loving God even if God takes our soul away.'"

Our Rabbis taught: Once the wicked government of Rome issued a law forbidding the Jewish people to study and practice the Torah. Rabbi Akiva continued publicly bringing people together and teaching the Torah... Rabbi Akiva was arrested and thrown into prison...When Rabbi Akiva was taken out for execution it was the time for saying the *Shema*. They ripped his flesh with iron combs... He said to his students: "All my days I have been troubled by this verse, 'WITH ALL YOUR SOUL', that I interpret as 'loving God even if God takes our soul away.' I never thought I would have a chance to experience it. Now I do." He said the *Shema* and held on to the word אֶחָד *ehad* (one) until he died.

A heavenly voice said "Happy are you, Akiva, because you soul has departed with the word *ehad*!"

Brakhot 61b

1. This is a hard story. What lesson does it teach?
2. How did Akiva give honor to the Jewish people?
3. How did Akiva show that God makes a difference?
4. How is this a story of *kiddush ha-Shem*?

zionist

Hannah Szenes (pronounced Shenesh) was born in Budapest, Hungary on July 17, 1921. She and her brother were raised by their mother after her father died. While attending public school she experienced anti-Semitism. She then began to attend an all-girls Protestant high school where one of her teachers was the chief rabbi of Budapest. It was his influence that encouraged Hannah to join *Maccabea*, a Zionist youth group in Hungary.

From the age of thirteen Hannah kept a diary, and at the age of nineteen, when she immigrated to Palestine, she wrote in her diary, "I've become a Zionist. This word stands for a tremendous number of things. To me it means, in short, that I now consciously and strongly feel I am a Jew, and am proud of it. My primary aim is to go to Palestine, to work for it." Hannah moved to Eretz Israel by herself. She went to an agricultural college and then joined a kibbutz called *Sdot Yam* near Caesarea, by the sea.

soldier

World War II had begun. Hannah was happy living in Palestine, but she could not give up on the Jews being killed in Europe. She felt the need to help them escape the Nazis. Hannah joined a group of Palestinian Jews who were being trained by the British army as parachutists. She was the first woman volunteer, and she joined the British Royal Air Force. Their mission was to go into countries that were controlled by Nazis and work with partisan groups there to fight the German army. A second mission was to save as many Jews as possible from concentration camps. In addition, Hannah was to help British pilots who had been shot down.

In March of 1944 Hannah parachuted into Yugoslavia. She spent three months living there, trying to find a way to sneak into Hungary. In June she and three others crossed the Hungarian border. Once in Hungary she was quickly captured by Germans and imprisoned in Budapest.

hero

After being captured Hannah was tortured repeatedly in the hope that she would reveal her secret communication codes. She never did. She was determined to stay true to what she believed in. They tried to get her to speak by capturing her mother and threatening to torture her in front of Hannah's eyes. She still would not give in. Her mother was later released unharmed.

Hannah never revealed her code to her captors. On November 7, 1944, Hannah Szenes was killed by a firing squad. She refused the blindfold and stared squarely at her executioners. She gave her life to save other lives and to protect the Jewish people.

kiddush ha-shem activity: happy is the match

Here is a poem that Hannah wrote after she parachuted into a partisan camp in Yugoslavia.

Happy is the match that burns and kindles the flames.
Happy is the flame that burns inside the hearts.
Happy are the hearts to know when to stop with dignity.
Happy is the match that burns and kindles the flames.

1. What is this poem about?
2. What does it say about *kiddush ha-Shem*?
3. When is sacrificing one's life a good thing?

kiddush ha-shem hero: hank greenberg

jewish baseball player

If you know some baseball history, you know that Sandy Koufax was a Jewish baseball player who did not play on Yom Kippur. If you've got a really good sense of baseball history, you know that Hank Greenberg was the "original" Jewish baseball player who did not play on Yom Kippur.

The Greenbergs kept a kosher home and sent Hank to Hebrew school. Like every other Jewish family, they were expecting college and then great success. They had high hopes for their son—he would become a professional man: a doctor, a lawyer or a teacher. When he decided to become a professional ballplayer, it was a disappointment, but in time his parents accepted his love for baseball and his need to play the game.

Hank graduated high school and enrolled in New York University, but devoted much more time to semipro ball. The Yankees watched Greenberg for a long time, but it was the Detroit Tigers who offered him a chance to play pro ball. He talked them into delaying for three years so that he could keep his promise and complete his college education.

being a first jewish baseball player

Hank started out playing triple-A ball in Raleigh, North Carolina. At first he didn't fit in. He told this story about that experience: "One day I was standing on the field when I became aware of a teammate walking slowly around me, staring. 'What are you looking at?' I asked. 'Nothing,' he said, 'I just never seen a Jew before.' The way it was said, he might have said, 'I've never seen a giraffe before.' I let him keep looking for a while, and then he said, 'I just don't understand it. You look just like everyone else.'"

In 1933 Hank was brought up from the minors to play for the Detroit Tigers. Now that he was in the

major leagues, the insults became a major thing. He told his biographer, "Everybody got it. Italians were wops, Germans were krauts, and the Polish players were dumb polacks. Me, I was a kike or a sheeny or a mockey. The only thing that bothered me was there were a lot of Italians, Germans, and Poles, but I was the only Jewish player who was making a name for himself, and so they reserved a little extra for me...."

yom kippur

In 1934 the Tigers were in a battle for the pennant, Hank was hitting .339, and September 10 was the both a critical game and Rosh ha-Shanah. Hank played and hit two home runs, and the Tigers won. Ten days later, on Yom Kippur, Greenberg did not play, and the Tigers lost. They went on to win the pennant, but they lost the World Series, however Greenberg became the first Jewish Most Valuable Player. In 1938 Hank came within two runs of breaking Babe Ruth's record, and in May 1940 he became the highest-paid player. He also was the first baseball player to enlist in the army and serve in World War II. Even though he could have been excused because of his age, Hank chose to do his patriotic duty. After the war, at age thirty-four, Hank returned to baseball.

class tells

Hank Greenberg is known for his redesign of the modern first baseman's mitt, making it into a huge trap. When Jackie Robinson, the first black baseball player, entered the league, Hank was one of the few players who was friendly. Jackie said, "Class tells. It sticks out all over Mr. Greenberg."

Hank Greenberg had a difficult time in professional baseball. He faced lots of anti-Semitism and faced it with dignity. He lived *kiddush ha-Shem,* bringing respect to the Jewish people.

In Talmudic times rabbi was not a job, it was something that people did after work.

Rabbis did not take money for teaching Torah, for helping people solve problems using Torah or for helping a person find inner peace. Rabbi Shimon ben Shetah was the best teacher in Jerusalem, and he was old and poor. During the day, to earn his living, he sold cloth door to door, and he taught hundreds of students at night. His students knew that he would not take money for his teaching, so they decided to buy him a gift.

They chipped in and bought him a donkey. They got the donkey from a non-Jew. To make sure that the deal was clear, they repeated to him the Jewish first rule of acquisition: "We give you the money. You give us to the reins to the donkey. When we pull on the reins and the donkey takes a step, the donkey, the saddle, the blanket, the bridle and even the fleas on the donkey are ours."

When they gave the donkey to their rabbi and showed him how to take care of it, a ruby fell out from between the saddle and the blanket. Rabbi Shimon ben Shetah told his students to return the ruby to the donkey seller. They told the rabbi, "Because we were clear about how we made the deal, the law says that the ruby is yours." The rabbi said, "The law is one thing, but *derekh eretz*, the right thing to do, says that you have to return it."

When they returned to the donkey salesman he was tearing his business apart, hunting for the ruby. When they returned it he made it clear that he knew the law and that it was theirs. When they still gave it back, he fell down on his knees and said, "God bless the God of Rabbi Shimon ben Shetah."

Jerusalem Talmud, *Bava Metzia*, ii. 8c

1. How is this a *kiddush ha-Shem* story?
2. How was Hank Greenberg like Rabbi Shimon ben Shetah? (How did he do *kiddush ha-Shem*?)

shiru l'adonai

value: shiru l'adonai

Shiru l'Adonai means "Sing unto God". Singing is a big way Jews connect to God and to one another. Consider this story.

David was a very busy king. He had almost no time for himself. During the day he took care of the people's needs. During every free moment he tried to squeeze in time to study Torah. David knew that the Torah would give him the wisdom he needed to rule well. Late at night he crawled into bed. Every night he hung his harp over his bed. In the middle of the night the north wind would begin to blow. The wind would move the strings. Slowly a melody would emerge. When that happened, David would wake up and sing with his harp. He would add words and create his psalms. These were David's prayers. He learned how to praise God by listening to his harp.

(Brakhot 3b)

Jews have always believed that music builds a holy connection. Today many people are creating new Jewish music and playing older Jewish music, too. They are using music in schools, camps, youth groups and services. They are playing and singing with their hearts in order to move other people and to build a connection with God.

¹ Sing unto the Eternal a new song: sing unto the Eternal, all the earth.

² Sing unto the Eternal, bless God's name; show God's salvation from day to day...

⁶ Honor and majesty are before God: strength and beauty are in God's sanctuary...

⁹ Worship the Eternal in the beauty of holiness: fear before God, all the earth...

¹¹ Let the heavens rejoice, and let the earth be glad; let the sea roar, and all its richness.

¹² Let the field be joyful, and all that is in there: then shall all the trees of the woods rejoice

¹³ Before the Eternal: for God comes, for God comes to judge the earth: God shall judge the world with righteousness, and the people with God's truth.

King David used this psalm when he brought the ark into Jerusalem. The ark was a special box with special things in it. These things gave the Jewish people help to remember their past story. Later, when David was dead, his son Solomon built the Temple. This was the house of God in Jerusalem. Then the Jewish people kept the ark in the Temple. A version of this story is found in 1 Chronicles 16:23-33. There we can read the story of David bringing the ark to Jerusalem by personally leading the singing and dancing.

1. How can the earth sing a song to God?
2. What is there to sing about?
3. Rewrite this psalm into a song. You can listen to the versions by Craig Taubman and Debbie Friedman.

shiru l'adonai hero: debbie friedman

Debbie Friedman changed American Jewish music forever. When talking about her life Debbie says, "I didn't get into Jewish music. It got into me." She explains, "The prayer has spoken to me, and I just sing back with my friends."

the early years

Debbie was born in Utica, N.Y. Her *bubbe* (grandmother) and *zadie* (grandfather) lived upstairs. When she was five years old her father decided to move the family to St. Paul, Minnesota. She first picked up a guitar at the age of sixteen, inspired by Barbara Gutkin, one of her fellow counselors at Herzl Camp in Wisconsin. At home she continued to teach herself how to play, mostly by listening to Peter, Paul and Mary records.

In 1968 she became a song leader for her synagogue's youth group. She attended a song-leading workshop at the UAHC Kutz Camp Institute in Warwick, N.Y. Her first song was a setting of the *V'Ahavta* that begins with the phrase "And thou shalt love the Lord your God...". "I taught it to a group of kids who were doing a creative service with James Taylor, Joan Baez and Judy Collins music. Not only did they sing the *V'Ahavta*; they stood arm in arm. They were moved; they were crying."

In 1972 Debbie recorded her first album, *Sing unto God*, a compilation of songs from the Shabbat service featuring a high school choir. "I had planned to make a demo tape, but when I found out it would cost only $500 more to make a thousand LPs, I thought, why not? They sold like hotcakes at camp. That's how it started. It was a fluke."

a career

Debbie's music has been influenced by sources as different as Judy Collins and the late Qwaali singer Nusrat Fateh Ali Khan. Debbie has created a library of music that is everywhere: the melody for *havdalah*, *Mi Sheberakh*, "The Alef-Bet Song", and more music that you probably know. Debbie says, "What I do is respond to text. A rabbi friend of mine calls my music musical *midrash*." She says, "In the text that I'm working on at the moment, one particular phrase goes over and over in my head. I write about what comes to my mind in relationship to these words, lyrically and musically." When she writes Hebrew texts into music the language practically writes itself, she says. "Hebrew has its own internal, passionate music."

Debbie has written hundreds of songs, recorded some twenty albums and sung with thousands and thousands of people, including four concerts at Carnegie Hall. Her music is sung all over the world. She is also on the faculty of the Hebrew Union College–Jewish Institute of Religion, where she helps to train rabbis and cantors.

a lifetime of work

Debbie Friedman's work is a product of her passion for "bringing people together" and the power of community united in song. "My objective is to involve people in the experience," she says. "I try to make prayer user-friendly. Because the music is in a familiar style, people are able to make the connection between the music and the text. The real power is in the poetry of the liturgy, how moving and stirring it can be, connecting us to our deepest and most precious ideas, hopes and fears." Debbie lives—and her songs spread—the value of *shiru l'Adonai*.

shiru l'adonai text: miriam's song

Here are the lyrics of one of Debbie Friedman's songs. It is about a time when women are singing.

CHORUS: And the women dancing with their timbrels
Followed Miriam as she sang her song.
Sing a song to the One whom we've exalted.
Miriam and the women danced and danced
the whole night long.

And Miriam was a weaver of unique variety.
The tapestry she wove was one which sang our history.
With every thread and every strand
she crafted her delight.
A woman touched with spirit, she dances
toward the light.

CHORUS

As Miriam stood upon the shores
and gazed across the sea,
The wonder of this miracle she soon came to believe.
Whoever thought the sea would part
with an outstretched hand,
And we would pass to freedom,
and march to the promised land?

CHORUS

And Miriam the Prophet took her timbrel in her hand,
And all the women followed her just as she had planned.
And Miriam raised her voice with song.
She sang with praise and might,
We've just lived through a miracle,
we're going to dance tonight.

CHORUS

1. Can you figure out what moment is being described in this song? What is it?

2. What feeling does this song create?

sing unto god

Music changes people's lives. What are some of your favorite songs? Favorite Jewish songs? When do you sing unto God?

shiru l'adonai hero: craig taubman

Craig Taubman's dynamic music and moving performance style have inspired the Jewish community for over twenty-five years. He brings the joy and spirit of Jewish heritage to life. Craig is a singer, songwriter, performer, album producer, event creator and worship leader. For Craig, *shiru l'Adonai* is a way of life.

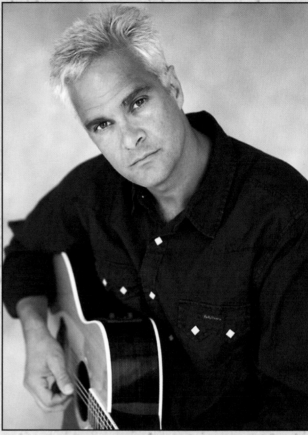

the start

Craig first began creating Jewish music at the age of fifteen, when he picked up a guitar and began to lead services at Camp Ramah in Ojai, California. He continued at USY and at Los Angeles Hebrew High School. Raised in Los Angeles to a Conservative Jewish family, his interest in music was interwoven with his passion for Jewish history and culture. Craig's path led him to record two albums for the Los Angeles Hebrew High School. He then founded Yad B'Yad, a city-wide teen performing arts program funded by the Bureau of Jewish Education.

secular success

Taubman's career took off when he became a Disney recording artist in the early 1990s. He was seen in heavy rotation on the Disney Channel performing songs like "Haircut" and in concerts like "Rock'n Toontown" at Disneyland. In recent years he has branched out into recording and performing more adult-oriented music, most of it Jewish in nature, although he continues to record and perform for children.

jewish success

Rabbi David Wolpe asked Craig to compose and perform a new erev Shabbat service for Sinai Temple. "Friday Night Live," held once a month at Sinai Temple in Los Angeles. It is matched with "One Shabbat Morning," which has also become a monthly service at Adat Ari El in Los Angeles. These two services have changed the nature of music in the Conservative Movement and inspired more and more congregations to create their own "Engaging Shabbat" experiences.

"I am happiest doing the Jewish stuff," Taubman says, "but my feet are firmly grounded in both communities." His life work sings to God. While Debbie Friedman brought folk music to Jewish services, Craig made them rock.

shiru l'adonai

Here is the song that Craig wanted you to look at.

Anim zmirot these songs we sing
Anim zmirot these song we weave
From where they come to where they go
Anim zmirot these song we sing.

1. What do you think *anim zmirot* means?

2. What does this song say about singing?

3. Where is God involved?

pikuah nefesh

Jews have an obligation to save another person. It is rooted in a principle of *halakhah* (Jewish law) called פְּקוּחַ נֶפֶשׁ, *pikuah nefesh*, saving a soul. Protecting a human life is a major Jewish obligation. Our rabbis learned this lesson from two different places in the Torah. Leviticus 19:16 says, "DO NOT STAND IDLY BY THE BLOOD OF YOUR NEIGHBOR." In a midrashic collection, *Sifra*, we are taught that "DO NOT STAND IDLY BY THE BLOOD OF YOUR NEIGHBOR" means "Do not watch without doing something when your neighbor's blood is shed. If you see someone in danger of drowning in the river, being carried away by wild beasts or being attacked by robbers, you must try to rescue that person." (Leviticus 19:16)

The second verse, Leviticus 18:5, reads, "YOU SHALL KEEP MY LAWS AND MY RULES, YOU SHALL ACT ON THEM, YOU SHALL LIVE BY THEM." The key words here are "LIVE BY THEM". In the Talmud we are told "You shall live by them, but you shall not die because of them" (*Yoma* 85a). This teaches a second meaning of *pikuah nefesh:* that one may abandon most *mitzvot* in order to save a life.

83

It was reported about Hillel the Elder that every day he used to work and earn one *tropik* (a small coin). Half of it he would give to the guard at the house of learning; the other half was spent for food for him and his family.

One day he found nothing to earn, and the guard at the house of learning would not permit him to enter. He climbed up and sat on a window to hear the words of the living God from the mouth of Rabbi Shemayah and Rabbi Avtalion. That day was the eve of Shabbat, also the winter solstice, and snow fell down on him from heaven.

When the dawn rose, Rabbi Shemayah said to Rabbi Avtalion: "Brother Avtalion, on every day this house is light, and today it is dark. Is it perhaps a cloudy day?"

They looked up and saw the figure of a man in the window. They went up and found Hillel covered by snow. They brought him inside, bathed and anointed

him, lit a fire, and placed him next to it. They said, "This man deserves that the Sabbath be broken for him." Lighting the fire violated the rules for Shabbat (*Yoma* 35a). "Break one Shabbat for his sake, so that he may keep many *Shabbatot*." (*Yoma* 85b)

This story is an expression of the Leviticus 18:5, which reads: "YOU SHALL KEEP MY LAWS AND MY RULES, YOU SHALL ACT ON THEM, YOU SHALL LIVE BY THEM."

What is the moral of this story?

pikuah nefesh hero: henrietta szold

Henrietta Szold was an amazing Jewish woman. She did serious academic work, was one of the first women to take a rabbinical education, started the largest Jewish organization in the world, created a major medical center, helped to start the State of Israel and worked for Jewish youth.

early life

Henrietta Szold was born in Maryland in 1860. She was the eldest daughter of a Baltimore rabbi. As a young girl she excelled in school. When Szold was in her early twenties Baltimore was flooded with immigrants fleeing poverty and persecution in Russia. They spoke little or no English and were unprepared for America. To help them adjust, Szold founded one of the first night schools. Many of her students told about the terrible conditions of Jews in Russia. Curious, she traveled Russia in 1881 and was alarmed at the distress. On that trip she became interested in *Hovevei Zion*, an early Zionist organization.

In 1902 Szold moved to New York City and enrolled at the Jewish Theological Seminary (JTS). This was before women were allowed to be rabbis. In order to participate in classes she had to promise never to ask to be ordained as a rabbi.

hadassah

Szold had a passionate belief in the ability of women to participate in the public world. With six other women she started Hadassah, originally a women's group that studied Zionist texts. Szold was the only one who had been to *Eretz Yisrael*. She had seen the poverty, illness and tremendous needs. "If we are Zionists, as we say we are, what is the good of meeting and talking and drinking tea? Let us do something real and practical—let us organize the Jewish women of America and send nurses and doctors to Palestine."

The women liked her idea, and in 1912 Hadassah was born.

Hadassah funded hospitals, a medical school, dental facilities, x-ray clinics, infant welfare stations, soup kitchens and other services for Palestine's Jewish and Arab inhabitants.

In 1918 the American Zionist Medical Unit headed to Palestine with forty-four doctors, nurses and other health care workers. They set up a hospital and trained members of the community to provide health care themselves. In 1920 Szold went to *Eretz Yisrael* to supervise the medical unit's work herself. She intended to stay for just two years, but she never permanently returned to America.

In 1934 Hadassah built a hospital on Mount Scopus in Jerusalem that quickly became the finest in the Middle East.

youth aliyah

Leaders recognized Szold's talent. In 1927 she was elected to the executive committee of the Jewish Agency. She was given responsibility for the health and social welfare of the community. She focused especially on the needs of children.

In the 1930s the Nazis in Germany and Austria were passing laws restricting Jewish rights, beating up Jews and sending many to concentration camps. Thousands of parents wanted to save their children by sending them to Palestine. To arrange for such an *aliyah* the Jewish community turned to Henrietta Szold.

She threw herself into the task of saving German Jewish youth. When each group of children arrived by boat at the port of Haifa, she greeted them personally. They were brought to villages, given medical care, food and housing, Hebrew lessons and job training.

When she died in 1945 the entire Jewish people mourned her loss. A child from the *Youth Aliyah* recited the *Kaddish* at her funeral. She was a woman who did a lot of *pikuah nefesh*.

Here is a speech that Henrietta Szold gave at dedication of the Hadassah Hospital, April 30, 1929.

Time will pass judgment upon the work of Hadassah done so far...Yet I dare to believe that when the history of the Zionist resettlement of Eretz Yisrael comes to be written the historian will have to say of the Hadassah undertaking: It began as a mere war relief measure. It stayed on in the land as an effective peace organization. It entered into the fabric of life in Eretz Yisrael, as a part of the renewal and rehabilitation Zionism stands for. From first to last, it remained true to its motto, "The healing of the daughter of my people."

1. What is Henrietta proud of?
2. What does she believe is the purpose of Hadassah?
3. In what ways did her work create *Pikuah Nefesh*.

hadassah

Henrietta Szold founded the woman's organization, Hadassah. Hadassah in turn created the Hadassah Medical Organization. This is what the organization says about its purpose.

Founded by Hadassah, the Women's Zionist Organization of America, the Hadassah Medical Organization pioneered the development of standards and practices of health care in Israel.

Its main focus and its health care activities are in Jerusalem. Its heritage and emotional links are deeply rooted in the land of Israel and its people.

Hadassah Medical Organization is also a bridge to peace. It forges links between its staff and patients of all nationalities, races and religions who heal and who come to its doors for healing.

1. What does Hadassah Medical Organization say about its history?
2. What is the main thing it does?
3. How does it work for peace?

pikuah nefesh hero: jonas salk

polio

Polio is a disease caused by a virus. Sometimes it does not cause serious illness, but sometimes it causes paralysis. It kills people who get it, usually by paralyzing the muscles that help him or her breathe. Polio used to be common in the United States. At the height of the polio epidemic in 1952, nearly 60,000 cases with more than 3,000 deaths were reported in the United States alone.

Very few can say that they cured a disease that killed people. But Jonas Salk could. That is real *pikuah nefesh*.

early years

Jonas Salk was born October 28, 1914 to Orthodox Jewish parents in the Bronx. He was the oldest of three sons and was the most observant. "My brothers called me the little rabbi," he said. He went to Hebrew school from the age of eight.

As a child he was thin and small and did not do well at sports. He was, however, an excellent student. His mother used to tell him he would make a difference by doing something significant.

Salk graduated from Townsend Harris High School, a school for exceptional students. He entered the College of the City of New York to study law, but he changed his mind and decided to go into medicine. In 1934 he enrolled in the College of Medicine of New York University, from which he graduated in 1939. Salk worked at New York's Mount Sinai Hospital from 1940 until 1942, when he went to the University of Michigan. There he helped develop an influenza (flu) vaccine.

Salk had an idea. He was going to develop a polio vaccine using dead bits of the viruses. That challenged medical practice, which held that only vaccines made of living viruses could produce effective, lasting immunity. To proceed with his work he had to hold onto a belief that was in the minority. He believed that this was something Jews had been doing for hundreds of years.

polio vaccine

In 1949 it was learned that there were three distinct types of polio viruses. This discovery provided a starting point for Salk. He prepared a dead virus vaccine effective against all three types. In 1955 the vaccine was determined to be safe for general use. The Salk vaccine is a series of three or four injections. When someone had the vaccine, that person was saved from polio. The Salk vaccine saved many lives and kept many people from paralysis. New York City wanted to honor Salk with a ticker-tape parade. He said, "No, thank you."

later

In 1963 Salk opened the Salk Institute for Biological Studies in San Diego, California. There he and his colleagues studied problems related to the body's autoimmune reaction (the method by which the body rejects foreign material). Jonas Salk died on June 23, 1995, in Los Angeles at the age of eighty. When he died both he and his Salk Institute were working toward a cure for AIDS (an autoimmune disease).

The work Jonas Salk did to end polio is real *pikuah nefesh*.

pikuah nefesh: study texts

Here are a series of texts that teach us about the Jewish understanding of being a life-saver.

DO NOT STAND ON YOUR NEIGHBOR'S BLOOD, I AM THE ETERNAL. (Leviticus 19:16)

Where do we know that if a person sees another drowning, mauled by beasts or attacked by robbers, that person is bound to save the other? From Leviticus 19:16, "DO NOT STAND ON YOUR NEIGHBOR'S BLOOD." *(Talmud, Sanhedrin 73a)*

Whoever is able to save another and does not save him breaks the *mitzvah* "DO NOT STAND ON YOUR NEIGHBOR'S BLOOD, I AM THE ETERNAL." Similarly, if one sees another drowning in the sea or being attacked by bandits or being attacked by a wild animal and is able to rescue him...and does not rescue him... [he] breaks the injunction "DO NOT STAND ON YOUR NEIGHBOR'S BLOOD, I AM THE ETERNAL."

(Mishneh Torah, Hilkhot Rotzeah, 1:14)

The Torah gave permission to the physician to heal. More importantly, this is a *mitzvah,* and it is included in the category of saving life; and if a doctor withholds services, it is considered an act of shedding blood.

(Shulhan Arukh, Yoreh Deah 336)

1. What is the meaning of "DO NOT STAND ON YOUR NEIGHBOR'S BLOOD"?

2. What does this verse mean for physicians?

3. What does it mean for you?

being prepared

If every Jew has an obligation to save life what are some of the things you should be prepared to do? What are some of the things you should do right now?

tzedakah

value: tzedakah

Tzedek means "justice". *Tzedakah* comes from *tzedek*. Charity is a matter of the heart. *Tzedakah* is an obligation. Even if one doesn't feel like it, Jews are supposed to give *tzedakah*.

The Jewish tradition has rules for *tzedakah*. One is supposed to give at least ten percent of one's income to *tzedakah*. No one is supposed to give more than thirty percent. These limits come from rules the Bible gives for Jewish farmers. One had to leave the corners of one's fields, anything dropped and anything forgotten to the poor to harvest for themselves. One had to take a portion of one's field and give it to God's purposes, including the poor.

The prophet Hosea teaches, "PLANT *TZEDAKAH* ON YOUR OWN AND YOU WILL HARVEST KINDNESS" (10:12). The *midrash* expands the idea by saying, "The poor person does more for the rich person than the rich person does for the poor." (*Exodus Rabbah* 34:8)

tzedakah text: bava batra 10a

Rabbi Akiva had a Roman friend named Tinnius Rufus.

Tinnius Rufus said, "You have a God who loves people and who cares for their needs. Your God wants the hungry to be fed and the homeless to be sheltered. God has the power to take care of all human needs. Why does God command you to share your wealth to take care of the poor rather than just making it good for all?"

1. If you were Rabbi Akiva, how would you answer your friend?

Rabbi Akiva answered: "The giving of *tzedakah* lets money become a means of creating holiness. God is the creator of both the rich and the poor. God wants all God's children to help one another. The giving of *tzedakah* makes the whole world into one loving household."

2. If you were Tinnius Rufus, what would you learn from Akiva's answer?

tzedakah maven: danny siegel

Danny Siegel discovers and tells the stories of *mitzvah* heroes. He has been called The World's Greatest Expert on Microphilanthropy, The Feeling Person's Thinker and The Pied Piper of *Tzedakah*.

the early years

Danny says, "My *abba*, Julius, moved to northern Virginia to set up a medical practice as an old-time country doctor. For more than a half-century he would treat, heal, cure, comfort and care for three generations of patients, thousands in all. I rode with my father often. I witnessed the kind of people he treated: kind people, simple people, people who would give you the shirt off their back, bring you in and feed you if you were hungry...In our community he was known as a *ba'al tzedakah*, a person who used his *tzedakah* money wisely.

"My mother, Edythe Siegel, was the classic *tzadeket*—not just because she was so involved in Sisterhood, Seaboard Branch of Women's League and Hadassah. She was wise, recognized needs, responded, cared..."

usy

United Synagogue Youth (the Conservative youth movement) changed Danny's life. He was chapter treasurer and president, regional treasurer and president and finally international president, and went on USY Pilgrimage (to Israel) in 1961. In high school, Danny felt the effects of learning differently/ disabilities, ADD (attention deficit disorder), and "poetic tendencies." He started but didn't complete, studies to become a rabbi. He holds a bachelor's degree in literature from Columbia and bachelor's and master's degrees in Hebrew literature from the Jewish Theological Seminary. In 1972 he became a traveling teacher and poet when he drove the Atid (Conservative college program) bookmobile around the country selling Jewish books.

traveling tzedakah

The rest started with "traveling *tzedakah*." It is a Jewish custom to give some money to a person going on a trip. That person becomes the *shali'ah* (messenger) for your *tzedakah mitzvah*. Some people believe that anyone who is *shali'ah mitzvah* will have a safe trip. "Rather than wait for people to give me a dollar, I began to ask for money and wound up with $955. When I got to Israel, I went in search for the right people and places to give it."

The search for the right people and places to distribute the money became an ongoing search for *mitzvah* heroes. Here are some of Danny's first finds:

- Hadassah Levi, who made her life's work the rescue abandoned infants with Down Syndrome.

- Myriam Mendilow, who found Jerusalem's poor, elderly residents on the streets of the city and gave them respect and new purpose in her program *Yad L'Kashish* (Lifeline for the Old).

- Uri Lupolianski, a young teacher who founded *Yad Sarah*, which lends medical equipment to those who need it.

In its twenty-seven-year history Ziv Tzedakah Fund, which Danny founded, gave more than $13,500,000 to *mitzvah* heroes and organizations. This money, for the most part, was collected in donations of $10, $18 and $25.

teaching tzedakah

Throughout the year Danny travels around teaching about *tzedakah* and Jewish values and reading poetry. Every summer since 1976 he has served as USY Israel Pilgrimage *Tzedakah* Resource Person. He is the author of twenty-nine books on *mitzvah* heroes, practical and personalized *tzedakah* and poetry.

Danny says, "There is nothing magical or mystical about it—nothing requiring two Ph.D.s or expertise in software. Just find some *mitzvah* heroes, find some money, work with them, give to them and be happy."

tzedakah text: a danny siegel poem

the good people

The Good People everywhere
will teach anyone who wants to know
how to fix all things breaking and broken in this world—
including hearts and dreams—
and along the way we will learn such things as
why we are here
and what we are supposed to be doing
with our hands and minds and souls and our time.
That way, we can hope to find out why
we were given a human heart,
and that way, we can hope to know
the hearts of other human beings
and the heart of the world.

1. Who are the "good people"?
2. Why are they here?
3. What is the heart of the world?
4. What is the lesson of this poem?
5. How does it connect *tzedakah* and *tikkun olam*?

pick a tzedakah organization

Here is a list of *mitzvah* heroes from **Mitzvah Heroes Fund, Inc.** (http://www.mitzvahheroesfund.org). Pick one hero and research him or her.

- **Avshalom Beni of HAMA** (http://www.hama-israel.org.il/). Israel's foremost animal assisted therapist.

- **Caryn Green of Crossroads** (http://crossroadsjerusalem.org/). Saving lives of English-speaking street kids in Jerusalem.

- **Dr. Menachem Gottesman of the Meled School** (http://www.meled.org.il/). The last chance for at-risk high school students.

- **Ruthie Sobel Luttenberg of Birthday Angels** (http://www.birthday-angels.org/). It provides birthday parties for children whose family can't afford one or are affected by terrorism..

- **Libby Reichman of Big Brothers/Sisters of Israel** (http://www.bigbrothers.org.il/) matches big brothers or sisters to children who need a mentor.

- **Zev Birger of Dental Volunteers for Israel** (http://www.dental-dvi.co.il/). Free dental clinic for Jerusalem's neediest children.

- **Phyllis Heimowitz of the Organization for the Emotional Support of Girlfriends of Fallen Israeli Defense Force Soldiers** (http://www.girlfriendsidf.org.il/eng/eng.htm). Helps girlfriends piece their lives back together after their boyfriends are killed.

- **Shmuel Munk and Yoram Mordechai of Bayit Cham** (http://www.bayit-cham.com/english/e-about.asp). Rehabilitates people with mental and emotional illness and depression via vocational training and job placement.

- **Linda Mosek of Click** (http://www.click-savi.org.il/). Making elders a productive part of a society.

- **Yitz Feigenbaum and Irit Zucker of Bet Hayeled** (http://www.bethayeled.org/). Helping to raise about ten kids in a warm and loving environment, and continuing to work with another eight "graduates".

tzedakah hero: natalie portman

Natalie Portman is an actor. She has been in many movies, such as *Star Wars: Episodes 1, 2 and 3,* and *Mr. Magorium's Wonder Emporium.*

early life

Natalie Portman was born Natalie Hershlag in Jerusalem on June 9, 1981. Her father is an Israeli doctor specializing in fertility and reproduction. Her mother now works as her agent. In 1984, when Portman was three, the family moved from Israel to the United States, where her father pursued his medical training. The family lived in Washington, D.C., and Natalie went to the Charles E. Smith Day School. Eventually the family settled in Long Island. Even though her family was not religious, Natalie continued at the Solomon Schechter Day School of Glen Cove, though she went to a public high school.

Portman graduated from Harvard University with a bachelor's degree in psychology. While attending Harvard she wrote a response to an anti-Israeli essay in the *Harvard Crimson.* At Harvard, Portman was Alan Dershowitz's research assistant. She continued with graduate studies at Hebrew University.

personal activities and beliefs

Portman serves as an Ambassador of Hope for **The Foundation for International Community Assistance** (FINCA International). It is a not-for-profit microfinance organization founded by John Hatch in 1984. FINCA is the innovator of village banking and micro-loans. Micro-loans are loans of under a thousand dollars (often as little as fifty dollars) that allow poor people to become entrepeneurs and start or grow their own businesses.

microfinancing

In 2003 Queen Rania of Jordan joined the board of FINCA International. After meeting with the queen, Portman became an Ambassador of Hope for the organization. Portman said about this meeting, "Because I'm Israeli and Queen Rania is probably the most high-profile Palestinian woman in the world, I had this dream of meeting with her and doing something that would promote peace and working together between Israeli and Palestinian women. She talked to me a lot about what she calls the 'hope gap' that exists between the one third of the world that has and the two thirds that do not. I wasn't even aware that two thirds of the world population are extremely poor, living on less than a dollar a day...It's not something they teach you in school in the United States." Portman has visited FINCA field projects in Mexico, Guatemala, Uganda and Ecuador and met with several members of Congress to argue for more government funding for microfinancing.

She explains microfinanacing this way: "In Uganda I met a woman named Efuwa who was one of the first clients of FINCA in Uganda eleven years ago. When she started the program she had ten children. Her husband was beating her, she was living on eighty cents a day and she was telling us how she would borrow dirty laundry water from her neighbors to clean her clothes because she couldn't even afford a little bit of soap. Now, eleven years later, she's opened up a restaurant. Her loans are up to $2,000 now because she's been such a reliable client. She hired seven other women. She sends all of her daughters to school. It's just amazing the amount of responsibility and pride that these women who have no education and virtually no hope can take with themselves with just a little bit of input."

Natalie Portman devotes a lot of time to Maimonides' highest level of *tzedakah,* helping people help themselves.

Rabbi Moses Maimonides was one of the greatest Jewish scholars of all time. He spent much of his time writing books that help Jews apply the laws and teachings of the Torah to the way they live and treat other people. In this text, from the Mishneh Torah, Rambam teaches that the levels of giving *tzedakah* are like the rungs of a ladder.

There are eight different ways of giving *tzedakah*—each way is better than the one that comes before it.

1. The lowest way of giving *tzedakah* is the person who gives *tzedakah* with a frown.

2. Above this is a person who gives directly to the person in need, but gives too little, even though the *tzedakah* is given cheerfully.

3. The next best case is the person who gives money directly to the person in need after being asked.

4. The next best case is the person who gives money directly to the person in need before that person has to ask.

5. The next best case is one where the person who receives the *tzedakah* knows who has given it, but the person who is giving the *tzedakah* has no knowledge of the person in need.

6. The next best way of giving *tzedakah* is where the giver knows who will get the money, but the person who receives the *tzedakah* doesn't know who gave it.

7. The next best way of giving *tzedakah* is where the giver doesn't know who will receive the money, and the person who receives doesn't know who has given it.

8. The best way of giving is to help people help themselves by entering into a partnership or helping them find a job.

No matter how it is given, giving *tzedakah* is a *mitzvah*.

1. Is there a bad way of giving *tzedakah*?
2. How is the best way different from the other ways?
3. How does Natalie Portman live the best way?

talmud torah

Talmud means "learning". *Torah* means both "the five books of Moses" and "instruction". Together *talmud Torah* stands for any kind of Jewish learning. In the *Mishnah* we are given a list of important *mitzvot*. Then it tells us "*Talmud Torah* is equal to them all." The suggestion is that it leads to them all.

We are told in the *V'Ahavta* that we should be constantly learning Torah, "when we lie down and when we rise up." This means that *talmud Torah* should be a way of life. Rabbi David Moshe was a Hasidic rabbi who said that once, during the dedication of a new *Sefer Torah*, he had to hold up a large, heavy scroll for a long time. One of his students offered to help, but he said, "Once you've picked it up, it is no longer heavy." This is a metaphor for Torah study. It teaches that once you get into Torah studying, it becomes easy.

While some Jewish schools are called *Talmud Torah,* Torah study is a lifelong learning process that goes beyond school. Learning Torah for one's whole life is a Jewish thing to do. Torah study is supposed to change us. It brings us closer to God, closer to our true selves and closer to one another. *Talmud Torah* is like being at Mt. Sinai and receiving the Torah from God.

talmud torah text: bava metzia 85a

In 132 C.E. Bar Kokhba led a revolution against Rome. He earned three years of freedom for the Jewish people. Then Rome struck back. Jewish life in Israel was all but destroyed by this Roman act of revenge. This story takes place right after that destruction.

Rabbi Hiyya and Rabbi Hisda were debating.

Rabbi Hiyya said, "If the Torah was forgotten, I know so much Torah that I could argue it back into existence."

Rabbi Hisda said, "When the Torah was forgotten, I planted and grew flax. I made a net out of the flax. I used the net to catch deer. I slaughtered the deer and fed the meat to orphans and used the skin to write a Torah. I taught Torah to groups of five and Mishnah (Oral Torah) to groups of six. I told them, 'Teach what you've learned to each other.' I made Jewish life normal again." That is how the Torah was brought back to the Jewish People when it seemed that there were not enough Jews to keep it going.

Bava Metzia 85a

1. What does Rabbi Hiyya say that Torah study is about?
2. What does Rabbi Hisda say that Torah study is about?
3. What do you think Torah study is about?

talmud torah hero: rebecca gratz

If you are reading this book in Sunday school, it is Rebecca Gratz's fault.

Rebecca Gratz is the one who invented the Jewish Sunday school. Her parents were observant Jews and active members of Philadelphia's first synagogue, Mikveh Israel. She was the first female Jewish college student in the United States. Rebecca Gratz was an observant Jew who devoted her life to the service of the less fortunate.

creating organizations

At twenty she organized the Female Association for the Relief of Women and Children of Reduced Circumstances in Philadelphia. She was its first secretary and the power house behind raising money. Gratz was also one of the founders of the Philadelphia Orphan Asylum and served as its secretary for more than forty years.

Sensing that there was also a need to service the needy and the unfortunate in the Jewish community she created a series of institutions: the Female Hebrew Benevolent Society in 1819, the Jewish Foster Home and Orphan Asylum in 1855 and the Fuel Society and the Sewing Society.

At the same time she did all of the charitable work, she also managed to raise the nine children of her sister, Rachel, who died in 1823.

the hebrew sunday school

After her sister Sarah's death in 1817 Gratz became concerned about Jewish education. Gratz saw a need for Jewish education among women and children. In 1818 she began a small religious school for her siblings and their children. At this point in history bar mitzvah preparation and private tutorials were the only path of formal Jewish education available for boys. There was nothing for girls.

In 1835 she urged the Female Hebrew Benevolent Society to create a Jewish educational program modeled on Christian Sunday schools that were successfully teaching thousands of children all over the United States. In 1838 the Society decided that "a Sunday school be established under the direction of the board, and teachers appointed among young ladies of the congregation." The school opened three weeks later, on Gratz's fifty-seventh birthday, with sixty students enrolled.

Gratz led the school for more than twenty-five years. She worked hard for the school, grading each student's homework and creating materials for the classrooms. Rebecca Gratz's grandniece, Miriam Mordecai, later remembered how family members had "helped 'Aunt Becky' paste little slips of paper over objectionable words or sentences" in books published by the Christian American Sunday School Union. The school was radically different from traditional Jewish schools; it was coeducational, and was taught in English. In addition, the school was run entirely by women. This was the first Jewish institution to give women a public role in the education of Jewish children. The model spread quickly. Women in Charleston, Savannah and Baltimore started their own Sunday schools.

Rebecca Gratz's work shows us the value of Talmud Torah by reminding us that every Jew deserves a Jewish education.

This story from the Talmud (Bava Batra 20b) tells the story of when it was made an obligation for a Jewish community to provide an education to every Jewish child. Previously the obligation was only for boys.

This Talmud text is written as a script. Read it and discuss the questions.

Narrator: Rabbi Judah taught us that Rav taught him this history lesson:

Rav: The name of the man who is to be blessed is Yehoshua ben Gamla. Were it not for him, the Jewish people would have lost the Torah.

[STEP 1] In the beginning, every son was taught by his own father. If a boy had no father, he did not learn.

Amora 1: Where in the Torah did they learn this practice?

Amora 2: They learned this practice from Deuteronomy 11:19:

Torah: And you shall teach them to your children...

Rav: [STEP 2] When this practice proved ineffective, because it left out lots of children who did not have fathers who could do the job, the Rabbis ruled that teachers of young children should be appointed in Jerusalem so that any young person could go there and learn.

Amora 1: Where in the *Tanakh* did they root this new practice?

Rava: They evolved it from the words of the prophet Isaiah (2:3):

Isaiah: *From Zion shall go forth the Law and the word of the Eternal from Jerusalem.*

Rav: When this was put into practice there was still a problem. If a child had a father, the father would take him up to Jerusalem and have him taught there. But if he did not have a father, he would not go up and learn.

[STEP 3] The Rabbis therefore ruled that teachers should be appointed in each region and that boys should enter school at the age of sixteen or seventeen.

But this still didn't work well because when teachers tried to discipline students that old, the students would rebel and then leave school.

Rivta: Why did they choose sixteen or seventeen? That seems foolish. According to Pirkei Avot 5:21, five or six is the right age to begin schooling. The problem was this: When there was only a regional school, it was considered too difficult and too dangerous for younger students to travel to another town.

Rav: [STEP 4] This is when Yehoshua ben Gamla ruled:

Yehoshua b. Gamla: Teachers of young children should be appointed in each town and neighborhood. This makes it possible for children to enter school at the age of six or seven.

1. According to Rav, how was Jewish education originally provided?
2. Why was the system changed?
3. What did Yehoshua ben Gamla order?
4. How was Rebecca Gratz's work like Yehoshua ben Gamla's teaching?
5. What did she change? What did she add?

talmud torah hero: nehama leibowitz

Jewish law says that a Jew is supposed to study the weekly Torah portion three times each week. Until recently few *parshat ha-shavu'ah* (weekly Torah portion) classes were given. Today there are *parshat ha-shavu'ah* class in almost every synagogue in the world. One woman is responsible. Nehama Leibowitz is a *talmud Torah* hero.

education

Morah Nehama (she would not let her students call her Doctor or Professor) was born in Riga, Latvia in 1905. In 1919 her family moved to Berlin, and in 1930 she received a doctorate from the University of Berlin, writing her thesis on German-Jewish translations of the Bible. That same year she made *aliyah* to Eretz Yisrael. She took a job at the Mizrachi Women Teachers Seminary, where she taught for the next twenty-five years. In 1957 she began lecturing at Tel Aviv University. She also gave classes at the Hebrew University in Jerusalem.

the gilyonot

From 1942 through 1971 Nehama sent out her renowned *gilyonot* (newsletters) on the weekly Torah portions. For that undertaking she was awarded the Israel Prize in 1956. At first Nehama would just pose questions about the Torah text and then respond to the answers sent in by students from all parts of the world and all walks of life. Nearly twenty years after the *gilyonot* were no longer circulated, her students were still sending in their replies to her questions, and Nehama, red pen in hand, would read them, comment on them and return them.

She once said, "I am excited by this vast army of old and young, mothers and girls, teachers male and female, clerks and laborers, veterans and newcomers of all communities, hundreds of thousands (literally) studying Torah for its own sake. For our joint studies involved no certificates, examinations, marks, prizes, no credits, scholarships, income-tax rebates, but simply the joy so deep of the one who studies Torah."

Eventually she expanded the question sheets into essays followed by questions. They were circulated in this expanded form. Then the pamphlets were collected into books, *Studies in the Weekly Sidrah*. Later these were reedited and organized by Torah portion, one volume for each of the Torah's five books.

Her approach to the Bible was an active one, and through her thought-provoking questions she demanded that her students adopt a similar active approach to the text. Her interpretations showed her vast knowledge of traditional and modern biblical commentaries. She sought to share with her students a love of the Bible as well as the belief that its levels of meanings were to be probed by all its readers. When asked to describe her methods, Nehama said, "I have no method...I only teach what the commentaries say. Nothing is my own."

In addition to her writings, Leibowitz regularly commented on Torah readings for the Voice of Israel radio station.

simplicity

Nehama lived simply and honestly. Her energies and such resources as she had were devoted to her studies and to her students, and they remain her legacy.

> The most important thing is that the students should study Torah from all angles; search it out, and choose or reject interpretations. All providing that they engage in Torah out of love.

She influenced three generations of teachers and students and made deep Torah accessible to anyone who wanted it. She died in 1997. Her tombstone reads simply, *Morah* (teacher).

talmud torah activity: nehama and the cab driver

Here is a story about Nehama and a cab driver told by Avigdor Bonchek.

A cab driver noticed that his passenger was grading papers, and he figured out that she was a professor of Bible. He took advantage of the ride from Tel Aviv–Jerusalem to ask a question that had bothered him for some time.

"What does Jeremiah (9:22) mean when he says: LET NOT A WISE MAN GLORY IN HIS WISDOM; AND LET NOT THE STRONG MAN GLORY IN HIS STRENGTH; LET NOT A RICH MAN GLORY IN HIS WEALTH. BUT LET HIM THAT GLORY, GLORY IN THIS: THAT HE UNDERSTANDS AND KNOWS ME"?

"Well," explained Nehama to her driver, "it means that human wisdom and human strength and riches are not really important values; the prophet is telling us that what really counts is knowing God."

"Yes, yes, I know," said the cab driver, with a trace of irritation, "but what does he mean when he says 'LET NOT A WISE MAN GLORY IN HIS WISDOM, AND LET NOT THE STRONG MAN GLORY IN HIS STRENGTH, LET NOT A RICH MAN GLORY IN HIS WEALTH...'"

Nehama tried again in her patient manner. "The prophet is teaching us a very important lesson in life. Those things that most men strive for riches, wealth and strength are—"

"Of course, of course. Understood!" interrupted the cab driver with impatience. "But what does Jeremiah mean when he says 'A RICH MAN, A WISE MAN'; but when he speaks of strength, he says 'THE STRONG MAN'?"

At this point in her story Nehama looked up with wide-eyed wonderment and a smile of admiration. "You know," she confided, "I never noticed that! That's a very interesting point!" Her message: When it comes to learning Torah, all Jews are equal, professor and taxi driver.

1. What was the cab driver's problem?
2. What was Nehama's answer?
3. When was a time you learned something in a surprising place?

index

a

Aaronsohn, Aaron 55
Abayudaya 39, 40
Abba Eban 67
Rabbi Akiva 72, 90
aliyah 45, 85, 99
Altneuland 43
American Maccabiah Games 19
American Zionist Medical Unit 85
Anavah 65, 66, 67, 69, 70
Anti-Defamation League 63
anti-Semitism 20, 21, 43, 51, 63, 64, 73, 75
Aquaculture 14
Arava 15
Auschwitz-Birkenau 31

b

Ba'al Tash'hit 11
Baeck, Rabbi Leo 49, 51, 52
Bar Kokhba 96
Bayit Cham 92
Beit T'Shuvah 61
Ben-Gurion, David 13, 14, 42, 46
Beni, Avshalom 92
Naftali Zvi Yehuda Berlin 42
Bet Hayeled 92
Big Brothers/Sisters of Israel 92
Birger, Zev 92
Birthday Angels 92
Borovitz, Rabbi Mark 61
Brackish Water 14
Brandeis, Justice Louis D. 55
Bratzlav, Rabbi Nahman of 17
British Royal Air Force 73
Buchenwald 31, 32
Bunam, Rabbi Simhah 65

c

Captain Compost 15
Catholic–Jewish relations 63

Central Association of German Citizens of Jewish
    Faith 51
Clergy and Laity Concerned about Vietnam 57
Click 92
Crossroads 92

d

Darfur 7, 8, 9, 31
Dembitz, Lewis 55
Dental Volunteers for Israel 92
Der Judenstaat 44
Dershowitz, Alan 93
Desalination 14
Disney 81

e

Einstein, Albert 67, 68
Eretz Yisrael 13, 19, 25, 43, 85, 86, 99

f

Feigenbaum, Yitz 92
Female Association for the Relief of Women and
    Children of Reduced Circumstances 97
Female Hebrew Benevolent Society 97
The Foundation for International Community
    Assistance 93
Four Chaplains Memorial Foundation, The 28
Four Chaplains, The 27, 28
Friedman, Debbie 78, 79, 80, 81

g

Gaon, Saadia 60
Gottesman, Menachem 92
Gratz, Rebecca 97, 98
Green, Caryn 92
Greenberg, Hank 75, 76
Growing in Sand Dunes 14

h

Ha'am, Ahad 42
Haas, Jacob de 55
Hadassah 37, 85, 86, 91
Hadassah Hospital 37, 86
Haifa Ethnological Museum and Folklore Archives 33
halakhah 49, 83
Heimowitz, Phyllis 92
Herzl, Theodor 43, 44
Heschel, Rabbi Abraham Joshua 57, 58
Hillel 18, 24, 40, 84
Hisda, Rabbi 96
Hiyya, Rabbi 96
Hochschule für die Wissenschaft des Judentums 49
Holocaust 7, 13, 29, 31, 38, 46, 50, 51, 52, 63
Hosea 89
Hovevei Zion 85

i

Israel Folktale Archives 33
Israel Declaration of Independence 45

j

Jewish Agency, The 85
Jewish Theological Seminary of America 57
Jewish Theological Seminary of Breslau 51
Jewish Council of Elders 51
Jewish Foundation for the Righteous 7
Jewish World Watch 7, 8, 9
Jonas, Rabbi Regina 49, 50

k

Kaddish 29, 85
Kamenir-Reznik, Janice 7, 8, 9
Katz, Noam 39
Kaungulu, Semei 39
Kibbutz Lotan 15
Kibbutz Sde Boker 13
Kiddush 30, 71, 72, 73, 74, 75, 76
Kiddush ha-Shem 71, 72, 73, 74, 75, 76
King, Martin Luther Jr. 57
Knesset 25, 45
Kol Yisrael Arevim Zeh ba-Zeh 35, 36, 37, 38, 39
Kook, Rav Abraham Isaac Kook 42, 70
Koufax, Sandy 75
Kraft, Robert and Myra 37–38

Krakow 63
Krayzelburg, Lenny 21, 22
Kristallnacht 49

l

Leibowitz, Nehama 99
Luria, Rabbi Isaac 36
Luttenberg, Ruthie Sobel 92

m

Maccabea 73
Maccabiah Games 19, 20, 21
Maccabi World Union 19
Maimonides, Rabbi Moses 94
martyr 27, 71
martyrdom 27, 71
Meir, Golda 45, 46
Meled School 92
mitzvot 10, 30, 53, 54, 83, 95
Mordechai, Yoram 92
Mosek, Linda 92
Moses 39, 62, 69, 70, 94, 95
Moshe, Rabbi David 95
Mount Herzl 25, 43
Mount Scopus 85
Muller v. Oregon 55
Munk, Shmuel 92

n

Nahmanides 54
National Water Carrier 13
Negev 13, 14
Nobel Peace Prize 25, 26, 26, 31
Noy, Dov 33, 34

o

Old-New Land 43
Olympics 19, 21
Ometz Lev 47, 48, 49, 50, 51, 52
Organization for the Emotional Support of Girlfriends of
    Fallen Israeli Defense Force Soldiers 92

p

Palestine 13, 19, 38, 41, 42, 43, 44, 46, 55, 73, 85
Papal Concert to Commemorate the Holocaust 63

parshat ha-shavu'ah 99
Philadelphia Orphan Asylum 97
Pikua<u>h</u> Nefesh 83, 84, 85, 86, 87, 88
Pirkei Avot 5, 66
Polio 87
Pope John Paul II 63, 64
Portman, Natalie 93, 94

q

Queen Rania of Jordan 93

r

Rabin, Yitzhak 25, 26
Reform 15, 39, 51, 57
Reichman, Libby 92
Robinson, Jackie 75
Rodef Shalom 23, 24, 25, 26, 27, 28
Ruth, Babe 75

s

Salk, Jonas 87
  Salk Institute for Biological Studies 87
  Salk Vaccine 87
Sanhedrin 66, 88
Schulweis, Rabbi Harold M. 7, 8, 9
Schwartz, Howard 34
Sdot Yam 73
shali'ah mitzvah 91
Shema 72
Shemayah, Rabbi 84
Sheta<u>h</u>, Rabbi Shimon Ben 76
Shiru l'Adonai 77, 78, 79, 81
Shmirat ha-Guf 17, 18, 19, 20, 21, 22
Shmirat ha-Teva 11, 12, 13, 14, 15, 16
Siegel, Danny 91, 92
Sizomu, Rabbi Gershom 39
Solar cooker 9
Szenes, Hannah 73
Szold, Henrietta 85, 86

t

Talmud 5, 7, 11, 22, 35, 36, 51, 69, 76, 83, 88
Talmud Torah 95, 96, 97, 98, 99, 100
Tanna de Be Eliyahu 66
Tarfon, Rabbi 5
Taubman, Craig 78, 81

Theresienstadt 49, 51, 52
Society for the Protection
  of Nature, The 11
Tikkun Olam 5, 6, 7, 8, 9, 10
T'shuvah 59, 60, 61, 62, 63, 64
Tzedakah 89, 90, 91, 92, 93, 94
tzedek 53, 57, 58, 89
Tzedek Tzedek Tirdof 53, 54, 55, 56, 57
Tzion 41
Tzionut 41, 42, 43, 44, 45, 46

U

UAHC Kutz Camp Institute 79
Uganda 39, 40, 43, 93
Uganda Question 43
United Nations 43, 57
United Synagogue Youth 91

v

V'Ahavta 72, 79, 95

w

Western Wall 63
Wiesel, Elie 31, 32
Wojtyla, Karol Jozef 63
Wolpe, Rabbi David 81
Women's Labor Council 45
World Zionist Congress 43

y

Yad Vashem 29
Yosef Yekutieli 19
Yom ha-Aztmaut 29
Yom ha-Shoah 29
Yom ha-Zikaron 29
Youth Aliyah 85

z

Zikaron 29, 30, 31, 32, 33, 34
Zionism 7, 41, 43, 44, 67, 86
Zionist 13, 15, 42, 43, 44, 45, 55, 67, 73, 85, 86
Zusya, Reb 62